Bo

M000210919

Leo Butler was born in Sheffield in 1974. His work includes *Made of Stone*; *Redundant*; *Lucky Dog*; *Faces in the Crowd* (Royal Court); *Devotion* (Theatre Centre); *Heroes* (National Theatre Education Tour); *I'll be the Devil* (RSC / Tricycle Theatre); *The Early Bird* (Queen's Theatre, Belfast / Finborough Theatre); *Juicy Fruits* (Paines Plough / Traverse Theatre / Royal Exchange Theatre, Manchester); *69* (Pleasance Courtyard, Edinburgh Festival); *Could You Please Close the Door Please* (FIND Festival / Schaubuhne, Berlin); and *Alison! A Rock Opera* (co-composed with Daniel Persad – Royal Court / King's Head Theatre / Spread Eagle Theatre).

Works by Leo Butler published by Bloomsbury Methuen Drama

Plays

The Early Bird

Faces in the Crowd

I'll be the Devil

Lucky Dog

Redundant

Collected works

BUTLER PLAYS: 1
(Made of Stone, Redundant, Lucky Dog, The Early Bird)

BUTLER PLAYS: 2
(Airbag, I'll be the Devil, Faces in the Crowd,
Juicy Fruits, Do It! 69)

Leo Butler

Boy

Bloomsbury Methuen Drama
An imprint of Bloomsbury Publishing Plc

B L O O M S B U R Y
LONDON · OXFORD · NEW YORK · NEW DELHI · SYDNEY

Bloomsbury Methuen Drama

An imprint of Bloomsbury Publishing Plc

Imprint previously known as Methuen Drama

50 Bedford Square	1385 Broadway
London	New York
WC1B 3DP	NY 10018
UK	USA

www.bloomsbury.com

Bloomsbury is a registered trade mark of Bloomsbury Publishing Plc

First published in 2016 by Bloomsbury Methuen Drama

Leo Butler has asserted his right under the Copyright, Designs
and Patents Act, 1988, to be identified as author of this work.

British Library Cataloguing-in-Publication Data
A catalogue record for this book is available from the British Library.

ISBN: PB: 978-1-3500-0467-2
EPDF: 978-1-3500-0468-9
EPUB: 978-1-3500-0469-6

Library of Congress Cataloging-in-Publication Data
A catalog record for this book is available from the Library of Congress.

Typeset by Mark Heslington Ltd, Scarborough, North Yorkshire

Contents

Boy was first performed at the Almeida Theatre, London, on 5 April 2016 with the following cast and creatives:

Abdul Salis   *Druggy Man, Andy on the Train, Security Guard, Lloyd, Policeman, Person in the Crowd*

Asiatu Koroma   *Schoolgirl (Madison), Teen in Supermarket, Person in the Crowd, Clubber, Commuter*

Bayleigh Gray   *Child in Doctor's reception, Mysha*

Demi Papaminas   *Schoolgirl, Homeless Girl, Person in the Crowd*

Duramany Kamara   *Teen Son in Doctor's reception, Toilet Attendant, Lamari, Person in the Crowd, Supermarket Shopper, Gym Member*

Ellie-Mai Gallagher   *Child in Doctor's reception, Mysha*

Emilio Doorgasingh   *Agitated Patient, Man with Dog, Exhausted Security Man, Policeman, Person in the Crowd*

Eugenie-Alexia Mulumba   *Schoolgirl #2 (Jada), Young Mum with Pushchair, Person in the Crowd, Clubber, Gym Member*

Frankie Fox   *Liam*

Georgie Lord   *Druggy Woman in Doctor's reception, Older Schoolgirl, Olivia, Student Doctor, Person on Train, Person in the Crowd, Sainsbury's Shopper*

Matthew Wellard   *Trendy Young Bloke, Homeless Guy, Jobcentre Advisor, Person in the Crowd, Jogger*

Mohammad Amiri   *Teenage Boy, Young Man on Train, Roadworker, Person in the Crowd*

Peter Temple   *Middleaged Man, Professional Man, Road Sweeper, Jobcentre Advisor, Roadworker, Doctor #2*

Ruby Bridle   *Schoolgirl, Homeless Girl, Person in the Crowd*

Sarah Niles   *Mum in Doctor's reception, Paula, Station Attendant, Jobseeker, Person in the Crowd, Commuter*

Teann McDonnell   *Schoolgirl #2 (Jada), Yong Mum with Pushchair, Person in the Crowd, Clubber, Gym Member*

Terina Drayton   *Schoolgirl (Madison), Teen in Sainsbury's, Person in the Crowd, Clubber*

Wendy Kweh   *Doctor #1, Fashionable Foreign Student, Jobseeker, Person in the Crowd*

Zainab Hasan   *Receptionist, Blonde Woman, Nat on the Train, Jobcentre Advisor, Person in the Crowd, Mother with Toddler*
Aeren Fitzgerald   *Patient in Doctor's Surgery, Person in the Crowd, EAS Claimant*
Angel Loren   *Sleepy Toddler*
Imogen Roberts   *Patient in Doctor's Surgery, Person in the Crowd, ESA Claimant*
Jenny Walters   *Mrs Charles in Doctor's Surgery, Woman with Pushchair, Person in the Crowd, Sainsbury's Shopper*
Lev Levermore   *Father with Child in Doctor's Surgery, Roadworker, Person in the Crowd, Dan on the Train, Olivia's Drunk Boyfriend*
Morgane Tapia   *Sleepy Toddler*
Osman Baig   *Patient in Doctor's surgery, Roadworker, Station Attendant, Bouncer, Sainsbury's Assistant, Person in the Crowd*

Director   Sacha Wares
Set designer   Miriam Buether
Costume designer   Ultz
Movement director   Leon Baugh
Lighting designer   Jack Knowles
Sound designer   Gareth Fry
Casting director   Amy Ball
Assistant director   Caitriona Shoobridge
Costume supervisor   Claire Wardroper
Sound associate   Benjamin Grant

Boy

Characters

Liam
Mysha
Doctor #1
Doctor #2
Schoolgirl #1 (Madison)
Schoolgirl #2 (Jada)
Middle-Aged Man
The Third Older Schoolgirl
Trendy Young Bloke
Blonde Woman
Man with Dog
Sainsbury's Shopping Assistant
Mum with Teenage Son
Teenage Boy
Paula
Policemen
Agitated Patient
Student Doctor (Rachel)
Young Woman (Livia)
Lloyd (Client Advisor)
Lamari
Professional Man
Uniformed Lady
Mother With Toddler
Sleepy Toddler
Roadworkers #1 #2 and #3
Young Muslim Man On Train
Homeless Teenage Girl
Uniformed Man
Exhausted Middle-Aged Man
Homeless Guy
Andy
Nat
Dan
Bouncer
Fashionable Foreign Student

Sports Direct Security Guard
Toilet Attendant
Policeman at Bus Stop
Dog
Woman with Pushchair
Druggy Man
Druggy Woman
Receptionist
Nurse
Client Advisor #1
Client Advisor #2
Client Advisor #3
Claimant #1
Claimant #2
Claimant #3
Sainsbury's Shoppers
Clubbers
Commuters
Young Woman's Drunk Boyfriend
Mrs Charles
Jogger
Woman at Gym
Young Mum with Pushchair

Other parts to be played by ensemble

All parts, except Liam, should be doubled or tripled, etc.

Small, non-speaking parts can be removed if necessary.

The play features scenes of simultaneous action and dialogue. These can be timed and, in some cases, trimmed, or even avoided if necessary. If possible they shouldn't be treated as 'background' scenes.

Setting

Present day – autumn/spring, definitely not summer or winter

Various locations in and around south-east and central London

Acknowledgements

Many thanks to Rupert Goold, Robert Icke, Lilli Geissendorfer, the amazing Almeida team, and the entire cast, creative team, and crew.

To Dominic Cooke, Howard Gooding, Anna Brewer, Carissa Hope Lynch, Dan Persad, Ramin Gray, Daniel Cerqueira, Nic Wass, Indhu Rubasingham, Brad Birch, Kenny Emson, and my family for all their support and encouragement along the way.

To Nazzi and Beatrice for everything and more.

And to Sacha Wares for seeing it, fighting for it, and for bringing it to life.

This play is dedicated to Ryan Milne.

1.

At the Doctor's.

Morning.

Doctor #1 *is sitting at her desk typing, and* **Liam**, *17, is sitting on a chair close by.*

Doctor #1 Right, so what can I help you with do you think?

Pause.

Liam Sorry, nah.

Doctor #1 That's okay.

Liam Yeah, I'm just . . . –

Doctor #1 No, that's fine, you take your time.

Liam Yeah, taking my time though init, Doctor?

Doctor #1 It's entirely confidential.

Liam Oh, what like you mean . . . ?

Doctor #1 Well if it's difficult for you. Whatever it is.

Liam Oh. Okay, cool.

Pause.

Liam Yeah, difficult.

Doctor #1 Right.

Liam Yeah, 'cause there was that like bare queue coming out the door though init? Everyone just piling out onto the street just now. Eight o'clock in the morning and I'm like 'nah, man'.

Doctor #1 Well, I deal with lots of kids your age if that helps. Young adults, I mean.

Liam Young adults then, wicked.

Doctor #1   There's not much that would surprise me I'm sorry to say.

Liam   No, I see that, I see that.

Doctor #1   Perhaps it would be easier if you wrote it down? I do have other patients to see.

Liam   Wicked, yeah, write it down.

The **Doctor** *slides a notepad and pen to* **Liam**'s *side of the desk.*

Liam   Oh, seen. What, like my name or something?

Doctor #1   No no, I've got your name.

Liam   Like my date of birth then sort of. My mobile number.

Doctor #1   Just whatever it is. Whatever you want to tell me.

Liam   Yeah, 'cause I've run out of credit? I've like actually run out of credit?

Doctor #1   On the pad.

Liam   What? – Oh, yeah, like . . .

Liam *takes the pen, leans over the notebook.*

Long pause.

Doctor #1   If it's making you uncomfortable.

Liam   Nah, sorry? Yeah, nah . . . –

Doctor #1   I take it you're active?

Liam   Yeah, active. What like athletics, gymnastics sort of?

Doctor #1   Sexually active.

Liam   Oh right, cool. Nah, I don't know maybe, yeah. Sexually then, okay.

Doctor #1   Because it's important you take precautions.

Liam   Precautions, cool cool.

Doctor #1   There has been a significant increase in STDs over the last ten years. I have kids coming to see me every day . . . – Young adults, I mean.

Liam   Nah, yeah I see that, yeah. Young adults.

Doctor #1   And if you are uncomfortable then we can try . . . –

Liam   Uncomfortable sort of, yeah. On the front stairs sort of.

Doctor #1   The front stairs.

Liam   Yeah, nah, the front stairs. Cold, like uncomfortable, miss.

Doctor #1   Right, so perhaps we should take a look at it then?

Liam   Oh. – What, you mean like . . . ?

Doctor #1   Front stairs, perhaps we should check for anything?

Liam   Yeah, wicked then.

Doctor #1   Lie down there for me. Would that be . . . ? –

Liam   Yeah, 'course 'course. Lie down there, you mean?

Doctor #1   Hop over there and we'll get you looked at, Liam, yes.

Liam   Oh . . . – So, like . . . ?

Doctor #1   Yes please.

Doctor #1 *moves and puts on latex gloves.*

Doctor #1   Okay?

Liam   Okay, yeah. So, down on this thing thing?

Doctor #1   Make yourself comfortable.

Liam   Yeah, like . . .

Liam *climbs up onto the bed.*

Liam   Cool, nah. Comfortable then.

Liam *positions himself, leaning on one arm.*

Liam   Oh, is that . . . ? –

Doctor #1 *adjusts* **Liam** *so that he's flat on his back.*

Doctor #1   That's fine, thank you.

Liam   No, thank you, yeah?

Doctor #1   And if you could just pull your bottoms down a bit?

Liam   Oh . . . –

Doctor #1   Not much, just towards the top of your thighs for me.

Beat.

Doctor #1   Just down a little.

Liam   Yeah, cool then cool, like . . .

Liam *awkwardly pulls down his trackie bottoms.*

Liam   Thighs sort of thing. Yeah yeah, like . . . –

Doctor #1   And I'm just going to take a quick look.

Doctor #1 *examines* **Liam***'s penis.*

Doctor #1   That's fine.

Liam   Fine, yeah, five inches.

Doctor #1   Hm?

Liam   Nah, just . . . Five inches init. Three four inches sort of thing. Like with the cold weather sort of? Funny.

Doctor #1   Good, and if I just pull the skin back?

Doctor #1 *takes* **Liam***'s penis and pulls the foreskin back.*

Beat.

Doctor #1 Right, okay . . . –

Doctor #1 *moves and removes her gloves, placing them in the bin.*

Doctor #1 Okay then, Liam, you can sit back up again then now.

Liam Oh . . . –

Liam *pulls up his boxer shorts, sitting up on the edge of the bed.*

Liam So like we're done then now?

Doctor #1 Well, you seem absolutely fine, I can't see any obvious signs of infection.

Liam Oh yeah, is it yeah? Fuck. Fuck, wicked.

Doctor #1 Well it's good to rule things out.

Liam Yeah, 'cause you're a doctor.

Doctor #1 I am a doctor, yes.

Over the next, **Doctor #1** *washes and dries her hands, then sits at the desk, typing/scrolling on the computer, as* **Liam** *climbs down off the bed and sits back in his chair.*

Liam Yeah, 'cause you know I like brought my sister here once? My little sister, she was sitting in this same chair I think, wicked.

Doctor #1 Come back in a week or two if it's still uncomfortable.

Liam Oh . . . –

Doctor #1 And I would suggest you pick up some of our literature on your way out.

You'll find lots of leaflets about safe sex, STDs, that sort of thing.

Liam Yeah, like the front desk by the stairs?

Doctor #1   That's right.

Liam   Nah, yeah 'cause there's two sets of stairs though init? Like I was like out there by the shops and I saw the queue? The ramp up the front, the waiting room, the queue on the front stairs?

Doctor #1   Queue on the front stairs.

Liam   Yeah, that bare queue out the front sort of thing just now.

Pause.

Liam   Sort of cold out there today I thought. Like the weather?

Doctor #1   Well, unless there's anything else?

Liam   Anything else then. Like anything else then, yeah?

Doctor #1   And perhaps you can decide what's bothering you next time.

Liam   Bothering me, 'course.

Doctor #1   If there's something wrong, something we can actually help you with.

Pause.

Doctor #1   It saves us wasting our time.

Liam   Nah, I can do that, cool.

Doctor #1   Cool.

Liam   Next time, yeah, nah, I'll . . . –

Liam *hesitates, then finally gets up.*

Beat.

Liam   So I should just ask for you at the desk then isit?

Doctor #1   Myself or one of my colleagues.

Liam   Yeah wicked, so I'm just like again. Sorry you had to go through that first thing.

Doctor #1   That's quite alright.

Liam *opens the door and makes to go through into the waiting room.*

Liam   Yeah, sort of just . . . –

Doctor #1   All the best.

2.

The surgery waiting room.

Liam *enters the waiting room from the* **Doctor***'s office.*

The waiting room is packed with **Patients***, along with a reception desk and* **Receptionist***.*

Liam *stops and hesitates as soon as he leaves the* **Doctor***'s office.*

He almost goes back in, but decides against it.

He moves through the waiting room, manoeuvring past **Patients***.*

He goes to the reception desk, but they are busy.

Telephones are continually ringing.

Pause.

Liam *looks at the leaflets on the desk – and randomly picks a few, stuffing them in his pockets.*

Pause.

Liam *makes to leave, then stops and uses the liquid handwash from the desk.*

Through the above, as **Liam** *passes through the reception, the following dialogues take place.*

A.

The Receptionist is dealing with a very Agitated Patient.

Receptionist   Well, you can't just turn up and expect an appointment, the doctors are fully booked for the day.

Agitated Patient   Isn't there a nurse I can see at least?

Receptionist   I'm afraid not, sir. And we don't make appointments over the desk any more, you should try and ring

B.

A Nurse enters, holding a clipboard.

Nurse   Mrs Ellie Charles? Ellie Charles?

Pause.

Nurse   Mrs Ellie Charles?

Pause.

C.

A Druggy Couple are waiting to be called. They've been waiting for a long time.

Druggy Woman   Fuck this shit.

Pause.

Druggy Woman   Over an hour man.

Pause.

Druggy Woman   Fucking bullshit.

Druggy Man   That's how long it takes.

D.

A Mum and her Teenage Son, in school uniform, who has a patch on his eye. He's playing a game on his phone, she's talking on her mobile phone.

Mum   – . . . doing better now they've got this new head-teacher init? Yeah, they all are, he's meant to be exceptional they say. Discipline, hm. You're telling me that's a good thing, they let them kids run wild. You can't let these kids run rings round you, that's what I've been saying my

between eight and nine o'clock in the morning.

Agitated Patient But I did call, I was kept on hold for forty minutes until I took the initiative and walked down here myself.

Receptionist I'm sorry, but you've missed the drop-in clinic and we can only make other appointments over the phone, that's surgery policy. If you come back tomorrow at eight o'clock . . . –

Nurse Ellie Charles.

Mrs Ellie Charles *stands and moves over to the* **Nurse**.

Nurse We'd save some time if you were to keep an eye on the board, Miss Charles, would you come with me?

Druggy Woman I swear I'm going to kill someone in a minute.

Long pause.

Druggy Woman Bitch came in after us.

Pause.

Druggy Woman Swear to god, bitch came in after us init?

Druggy Man Yeah, and she's like eighty or some shit.

Druggy Woman How long we been here already?

whole life. Yeah, and they need telling . . . Well, yeah, setting an example, who else is going to do that? Whole school, the federation . . . Well, you know it was in special measures don't you? – (*to* **Teenage Boy**) Sit back, stay in your chair.

The **Teenage Son** *doesn't, the* **Mum** *hits him on the arm.*

Mum – Sit back in your chair, David, come. (*Then back on the phone.*) The ofsted, you know? They see these kids running around,

Agitated Patient   Well, what about later today? Maybe someone's cancelled?

Receptionist   You can queue up at the drop-in like everyone else.

Agitated Patient   So there's nobody at all I can see? It's fairly urgent.

Receptionist   Would you like to tell me what the problem is?

Agitated Patient   No, I'd like to see a doctor.

Receptionist   Perhaps it's something you can ask a pharmacist about.

Pause.

Druggy Woman   Fucking hell, Michael, don't breathe on me like that . . . –

Druggy Man   Go private then.

Druggy Woman   Huh?

Druggy Man   That's why them go private. In and out.

Druggy Woman   Swear to fuck I'd go private. Private they don't fuck you over. You know if I was like Kate Middleton?

fighting, answering back, and . . . And the teachers let them do it, because they don't have the experience, because they give them the benefit of the doubt instead of just . . . – Yeah, I know that, instead of just dealing with the problem and giving them a slap round the head or taking away their phones when they need it. No, right, they should slap them round the head, this is life we're dealing with, it's their future. Give him what he needs if it means he gets the grades. No, it's in their interest too, that's their

Agitated Patient No, . . . A pharmacist? No, it's about my results I told you that.

Receptionist Results?

Agitated Patient Yeah, my . . . –

Agitated Patient passes the Receptionist a letter.

Agitated Patient These – this letter they sent me, the results from my . . . –

The Receptionist reads the letter.

Agitated Patient Look, I just wanted to

Druggy Man You aint.

Druggy Woman What?

Druggy Man You aint Kate Middleton.

Pause.

Druggy Man Dirty up the seat no – man, come. There's like kids n'shit.

job. Wouldn't bother sending him nowhere if that's the case, might as well stay at home. It's their job to make sure he leaves school with something under his belt otherwise . . . – Ha, no. No, he's alright I suppose. Trying to get round me now init? Trying to act like he had no part in it, yeah. Looks like *Pirates of the Caribbean* with his patch. – (*To the* **Teenage Son.**) Yeah, you're well enough to play that rubbish though init? – (*Back on the phone.*) No, I don't know, Pixelgram or something, Pixelgramt.

talk them through with someone. Today preferably.

Receptionist These are blood results aren't they? From Kings?

Agitated Patient
Yes . . . – No, that's actually confidential.

Receptionist I'd imagine you'd be better off going back to Kings.

Agitated Patient But you referred me there in the first place.

Receptionist I'm sorry . . . –

– (*To the* **Son**.) Sit up back in your chair. – (*Back on the phone.*) Yeah, well hopefully. Hope be to god.

Agitated Patient
Look, it says that they sent a copy of this letter to my GP, look.
Someone here must have got it, there must be someone . . . –

Receptionist Who referred you, sorry?

Agitated Patient I can't remember, whoever saw me last time.

Receptionist Ah . . . –

Agitated Patient
Whichever doctor was free that day, I don't remember the name.

Receptionist Well, the soonest we can get you in is probably going to be a couple of weeks now to be honest.

Agitated Patient Well, a couple of weeks doesn't help me does it? Five minutes, that's all. If there's someone who can just help me interpret . . . –

Receptionist Like I say, get the 68 to Kings, that's your best bet.

Long pause.

Druggy Woman Burning up. Why'd they turn the heating up so high?

Druggy Man Fuck knows.

Druggy Woman Why don't you know?

Liam (*to* **Receptionist**, *of the ringing telephone*) Sorry, should I like get that for you? Just the phone there, yeah?

Liam hesitates, then exits.

3.

A bus stop.

Morning

An unkempt **Middle-Aged Man** *is sitting on the bench, with two plastic bags by his feet. One bag is full of groceries, another is full of cans of lager.*

He is drinking discreetly from an opened can.

Pause.

Liam *enters, bag over his shoulder.*

He sits on the opposite end of the bench to the **Middle-Aged Man**.

Liam *hesitates, then rummages into his pocket.*

He pulls out two or three leaflets that he's taken from the Doctor's – one for rheumatoid arthritis, one for breast cancer screening, one for Parkinson's disease.

He folds one of the leaflets open and, absently, looks at the pictures and diagrams inside.

Pause.

The **Middle-Aged Man** *takes another sip from his can.*

He and **Liam** *exchange eye contact for a moment.*

Middle-Aged Man   Going to be a long wait.

Liam   Oh – What really then, yeah?

Middle-Aged Man   Yeah, really.

Liam   Yeah yeah, cool, I can see that.

The **Middle-Aged Man** *sips his drink, then tucks it into his jacket out of sight.*

Liam   Cool, yeah.

Liam *folds away the leaflets and stuffs them in his pocket.*

The **Middle-Aged Man** *takes his can out again and drinks.*

Very long pause.

Two **16-Year-Old Schoolkids** *on their way to school, both on their phones, walk past quickly, chatting enthusiastically while, at the same time, a* **Trendy Young Bloke** *enters from another direction. He is talking on his iPhone through a wireless headset, headphone in one ear, sipping a coffee.*

Trendy Young Bloke   Piss, mate, I told you . . . No, I told you last night, you can make your own way there . . . Mm . . . Mm-hm – Yeah and that's the advantage of being freelance isn't it? . . . No . . . No, I'm still here . . . – Well, it's three minutes according to Busmapper, but you know? That was ten minutes ago . . . –

Liam *watches the* **Trendy Young Bloke**, *and takes his own mobile phone out, fiddling with the buttons – although it has no power.*

Trendy Young Bloke   Well, you better get a move on then, I told you last night . . . – No, mate, I told you last night . . . – Mate . . . Mate . . . Piss, mate, I did. I told you last night what time it started, don't whin. . . . – When you and Toby were on Call of Duty, I came in . . . – Yes I did, I came in and told you not to stay up playing that shit all night . . . – No, it's a screening . . . It's an industry screening, you dick-cheese . . . Free drinks, wall-to-wall gash, it's Bafta . . . –

16-Year-Old Schoolgirl   Arr, this same TalkTalk advert again now. Why do they do that? They must know it just pisses everyone off having to sit through this shit? Just skip to the video man, what's wrong with you? Every time, look, even when you press replay, that's like another thirty seconds of waiting.

As he talks, the **Trendy Young Bloke** *moves away from the bus stop and starts walking down the road.*

Unnoticed by the **Trendy Young Bloke**, **Liam** *gets up off the bench and follows him at a short distance.*

Trendy Young Bloke (*continued*)   – . . . Bafta, Piccadilly – yeah, I know that, fuck off.

. . . – No, you don't have to wear a suit, no-one wears suits any more, just . . . – Funny, yeah . . . – Yeah, wear your hoodie, mate, that'll do it, your jail jeans . . . – Yeah, I know, that's what you get . . . – That's what you get when you move out to the arse end of Deliverance country . . . – Practically Croydon, yeah. (*Laughs.*) 'Squeal for me boy!'

Trendy Young Bloke *laughs, still walking.*

Liam *also laughs, still following.*

Through the next section, **Liam** *– as he follows – reaches in his pocket and unravels a tangled set of plug-in headphones. He pops one of the headphones in his ear.*

Trendy Young Bloke   – Christ, you're an arsehole . . . – I said you're degenerate, yeah you. You're a Lanister . . . – You're Joffrey Lanister, mate, you're incest spawn . . . – Where? – No, I'm still here now aren't I?
. . . I'm on Croxted Road, I'm going to try down by the junction, the thing, the Busmapper . . . – Who, Tess? . . . – I thought she'd left hours ago. . . . . – Well, get her out of there then, using up all the hot water. – . . . It's half past twelve, you homosexual, yes . . . Yes . . . –
Alright, get her out the shower, give her one . . . – Yeah, that's right, mate. Get her out the shower, schtupp her one-time up the batty and call an Uber . . . –

The **Trendy Young Bloke** *stops walking, so does* **Liam**.

Trendy Young Bloke   Yeah, piss mate, alright . . . – Yeah, alright alright, . . . –

Alright, mate, fine, 'you had me at hello' . . . –

The **Trendy Young Bloke** *turns and walks back the way he came.*

Liam *also turns and follows him.*

Trendy Young Bloke   Yeah, you and your mother . . . Your mother's HIV medication, yeah, ten minutes . . . – I'll be ten minutes, call an Uber . . . – Ten minutes, I'll be outside . . . –

Outside, mate, yeah.

4.

The third-floor balcony/walkway of an estate.

Day.

Numbers 22, 23 and 24 – adjacent flats.

The window of 22 is open. Through the window, a **Blonde Woman** (*Romani*) *in bra and tracksuit bottoms is standing by the sink, holding a dirty oven rack and scrubbing the grease off it with a soapy sponge. Music playing from her flat.*

The curtains are shut in the window of number 23.

Liam *enters, headphones plugged in his ears, bag over shoulder.*

He walks down the walkway to the door of number 23.

He rings the doorbell of number 23.

No sound.

Pause.

He rings the doorbell again.

Long pause.

Liam *knocks the letterbox on the door – rat-a-tat-tat.*

He waits.

The **Blonde Woman** *notices* **Liam** *and watches him from her window.*

Pause.

Liam *rattles the letterbox again – rat-a-tat-tat.*

He waits.

Pause.

Liam *bends down and peers through the letterbox as the* **Blonde Woman** *at Number 22 peers through her window, still scrubbing the oven rack.*

Blonde Woman   You looking for someone?

Liam   Yeah, like this is his place init? Lamari.

Blonde Woman   Who?

Liam   Yeah piss mate, Lamari.

Blonde Woman   Oh, he's gone out I think.

Liam   – Oh, cool then, has he? Sorry, right . . . –

Blonde Woman   I think you might have just missed him, darling.

Liam   Yeah, bra sort of.

Blonde Woman   What?

Liam   Nah, cool then. In that bra sort of.

Blonde Woman   You want to come back later, they're usually in around lunchtime.

Liam   Yeah yeah, I knew that, I was on the phone.

Blonde Woman   Well, I don't reckon he'll be far. Probably took the dogs to the park.

That's their shit all over the lift on your way up.

Liam   Try the park though init then?

Blonde Woman   Yeah, you could do that.

Liam *makes to speak, hesitates.*

Pause.

Liam   So like you're alright like that.

Blonde Woman   I'm what, sorry?

Liam   I said you're alright like that then too. Out the shower sort of thing.

Blonde Woman   What?

Liam   Nah, just . . . –

Blonde Woman   Who's out the shower?

Liam   Yeah, wicked, like you come out the shower sort of thing?

Blonde Woman   Ah, bless. You never seen a pair of tits before have you? Should

keep my blinds down from now on then, eh?

Liam   Oh . . . – What then, really?

Blonde Woman   Get out of it, go on.

Liam   Oh . . . –

The **Blonde Woman** *laughs.*

Liam   Sorry, nah . . . –

Blonde Woman   Well, I'll tell them you were looking for him then.

The **Blonde Woman** *shuts the window, and moves away, out of sight.*

Pause.

Liam *hesitates, then turns back to the door of 23.*

Makes to ring the doorbell . . .

Doesn't.

Pause.

Liam *moves carefully to the window of 22.*

He looks through the window, peering in.

Pause.

Liam *quickly exits back down the walkway.*

5.

The park. A woody, secluded spot.

Day.

A narrow path, bordered with clusters of trees.

A spot where a fire has been built, with empty cans and other rubbish.

Logs purposely placed as makeshift seats.

Liam *enters quickly, bag over shoulder.*

He moves into the cluster of trees, and drops his bag on the floor.

He hurriedly pulls down the front of his trackie bottoms.

He masturbates.

Long pause.

A **Man with a Dog** *(on a leash) enters. He is in a tracksuit, and carries a rucksack.*

He moves to one of the logs and sits.

He takes off his rucksack and opens it.

From the rucksack, the **Man with a Dog** *removes the dog's drinking bowl and a bottle of water.*

He proceeds to fill the bowl with the water, which the dog laps up.

By now, **Liam** *has noticed the* **Man with a Dog** *and has pulled up his trackie bottoms and turned round, still partially hidden by the trees.*

Pause.

Man with a Dog   She gets thirsty.

Liam   Nah, yeah.

Beat.

Liam   Yeah, nah.

Man with a Dog (*to the dog*)   Get thirsty, girl, don't you, eh?

The dog drinks, the **Man with a Dog** *strokes it.*

Man with a Dog (*stroking/fussing the dog*)   Yeaaaaaaah, that's it, girl, that's it.

Long pause.

Man with a Dog   She won't bite.

Liam   Eh?

Man with a Dog   Said she won't bite.

Liam   Oh, isit?

Man with a Dog   Well, not unless I tell her to anyway.

The **Man with a Dog** *starts to roll a cigarette with liquorice papers.*

Liam *moves out of the cluster of trees and walks towards the dog.*

Pause.

Liam *strokes the dog.*

Pause.

Liam   Leave shit everywhere though init?

Man with a Dog *gives* **Liam** *a look.*

Liam   Nah, just . . . – Dogs. They like piss and shit everywhere.

Man with a Dog (*to the dog*)   Arrr, who's this then, girl? Who's this creeping around the bushes on his own then, eh? Do we need to have a word?

Liam *stops stroking the dog, as the* **Man with a Dog** *lights his roll-up.*

Pause.

Man with a Dog   Get yourself a girlfriend or something.

Liam   Oh . . . –

Man with a Dog   Don't want to go blind.

Liam   Nah, I won't.

The **Man with a Dog** *begins putting away the dog's water bowl.*

Liam *picks up his bag and makes to go, as a woman in a tracksuit and cap, smoking a cigarette walks past them.*

Pause.

Liam   Nah, I will I mean.

6.

Bus stop (from Scene 3).

Mid-afternoon, about half past three.

Two Schoolgirls, *in uniforms, about 15 years old, are sitting on the bench of the shelter.*

They each have smartphones in their hands.

Schoolgirl #2 *has a box of fried chicken and chips on her lap, from which she eats throughout the scene.*

They are in mid-dialogue as the scene begins.

A **Third Older Schoolgirl** (*from a different school, with a different-coloured blazer*) *is standing under the shelter, close to the other two, reading a book, but also with her smartphone in her hand.*

A **Teenage Boy** *is standing just outside and leaning on the advertising hoarding (advertising the Lottery or a loan company).*

He has a bag on his shoulder. He is smoking a small joint.

Three or four **Commuters** *could also be standing or leaning around the bus shelter, waiting for the bus, looking at or talking on their phones, or staring up the road in anticipation of the bus.*

At some point through the schoolgirl banter, **Liam** *enters, bag over shoulder. He wants to get to the bench in the shelter, but it's taken up.*

Pause.

Liam *looks up at the bus stop sign.*

Liam *looks up the road for any sign of a bus.*

He leans on the side of the shelter, close to the two **Schoolgirls***.*

To repeat, the scene begins IMMEDIATELY with the following dialogue, with **Liam** *entering the scene some way through the* **Schoolgirls'** *banter and eventually making his way over to them when he finally speaks, thus . . .*

Schoolgirl #2   I just told you man, shut up, I don't even see him hardly ever.

Schoolgirl #1   Oh my god, you are such a liar. He's your cousin.

Schoolgirl #2   Half-cousin.

Schoolgirl #1   Bitch, you are posting on his wall every day. You're on his Instagram, Snapchat, you're on Twitter.

Schoolgirl #2   No.

Schoolgirl #1   Like every day, and you're telling me you can't DM him for me?

Schoolgirl #2   Nah, shut up, I never use Twitter.

Schoolgirl #1   Never use Twitter? Oh my god, you are such a lying bitch.

Schoolgirl #2   Why, because I'm not bff's with my half-cousin who I hardly ever see except at Christmas? 'Ask him to come meet me' – shit, my cousin don't even know you, cuz. You think just because you both happen to follow Sia and Ellie that he's going travel across town to meet you outside Costcutter? The man's twenty flipping two, he'd get arrested for even looking at some fifteen-year-old bitch with all that narsty shit in your hair.

Schoolgirl #1   Yeah, so why all the notifications from him then? Why's he posting pictures of himself with his top off?

Schoolgirl #2   Oh my god, because he posts them on his wall?

Schoolgirl #1   Shut up, they came through on my profile last night.

Schoolgirl #2   Yeah, because some other bitch retweeted them, dumbarse, check your phone.

Schoolgirl #1 *laughs, snaps a photo of* **Schoolgirl #2** *as she's eating.*

Schoolgirl #2 *(laughs)*   Hey, the fuck you doing?!

Schoolgirl #1   Yeah? Well, let me post this on my wall then. Hashtag lying-fat-bitch.

Schoolgirl #2   Madison, no . . . –

Schoolgirl #1   Hashtag Adele.

Schoolgirl #2 *(tries to grab the phone)*   For fucksake, don't be posting that, Madison, I swear to god I will high-five your face.

Schoolgirl #1   But I like this picture.

Schoolgirl #2   Shut up.

Schoolgirl #1   You with your bare greasy lips telling me my business while you stink out the bus stop with that narsty box of Morleys. You know that's probably like some three-week-dead rat or something?

Liam   Three-week-dead dog.

Schoolgirl #1   Yeah, dog, that's what they put in it, three-week-dead poodle. – You know I swear to god this bus.

Schoolgirl #2   I swear to god your face. Didn't I tell you we should get the 322?

Liam   Yeah, like Jamal and Lamari and everyone.

Schoolgirl #1   Who?

Liam   Nah, just Raphael's little sister. You're like Raphael's little sister though init? Like Aisha?

Schoolgirl #2   Aisha?! Oh my gosh . . . –

Schoolgirl #1   Duh, hello? My name's Madison.

Schoolgirl #2   No no, wait, he thinks you're Aisha fam! Like special needs Aisha with the googly eyes?

Liam   Nah, I don't know, like you were like in them year below us then, fam.

Schoolgirl #1   I aint your fam.

Liam   Nah, yeah, not your fam, –

Schoolgirl #1   Do I know you?

Schoolgirl #2   The 322, man, come.

Liam   Nah, yeah, we used to like get you vexed all the time? At break-time, Jamal and everyone, you were in the year below us, like . . . –

Schoolgirl #1 *takes a picture of* **Liam**.

Liam   Sorry, yeah, cheese.

Schoolgirl #1   What?

Liam   Nah, cheese then I think.

Schoolgirl #2   Oh my god.

Schoolgirl #1 *taps/scrolls, posting Liam's picture on Instagram. All the* **Schoolgirls**, *and* **Schoolboy**, *over the next section are looking at their phones.*

Liam   Yeah just, like Raphael n'ting, we were in Year Eleven?

Schoolgirl #1   Yeah, I know them boys.

Schoolgirl #2   Shut up, no you don't.

Schoolgirl #1   No, Jamal and Lamari, yeah, they like had a little thing for me init?

Everywhere I went they'd be following me around, bussin' convo, asking me out . . . –

Schoolgirl #2 (*looking at her phone, laughing*)   Oh my god, Madison, are you serious?

Hashtag Nemo?

Third Older Schoolgirl   Hashtag Paedo.

Schoolgirl #2 *dials a number on her mobile.*

Schoolgirl #1   Yeah, I used to hang with all them boys. Jamal, Raphael . . . –

Liam   Raphael, yeah, 'cause they're like my G's though? Kieran, Lamari . . . –

Schoolgirl #2 (*on the phone*)   Yo, Nelson, check your Insta.

Liam   – Orlando, Jamal . . . –

Schoolgirl #1   Yeah, I know them, I don't remember you.

Liam   No, but I remember you.

Third Older Schoolgirl   She's fourteen, mate.

Schoolgirl #1   The fuck am I fourteen, you don't know me. Jamal, Raphael or whoever, they were all like holding out for me.

Schoolgirl #2 (*on the phone*)   – Oh my god, you are savage, brov.

Schoolgirl #2 *ends the call, and starts tweeting/scrolling again. The* **Third Schoolgirl** *also checks her phone – scrolling on her Twitter feed, as . . .*

Schoolgirl #1 (*to* **Liam**)   Lamari, he was like all over me one-time, like – all over me?

You know he's a drug addict now don't you?

Liam   Oh . . . – Nah nah . . . –

Third Older Schoolgirl (*to* **Schoolgirl #2**, *of the Twitter feed*)   That is seriously out of order.

Schoolgirl #2   So?

Schoolgirl #1   Yeah boy, Lamari's like a serious drug addict now, I've seen his face – like it's well haggard?

Schoolgirl #2   G's bulimic, you idiot.

Schoolgirl #1   Shut up.

Schoolgirl #2   You shut up. Lamari Garner's bulimic, fam. Like he sicks up his food?

Schoolgirl #1   According to who, your idiot cousin with his bare faggot abs?

Schoolgirl #2   No, because there were three Lamaris init? Lamari he's talking about goes some technical college. He's like bulimic or depressed or abused or whatever.

Schoolgirl #1   Nah, that's the other Lamari.

Schoolgirl #2   Which other Lamari? There were three of them in the same year, bitch.

Schoolgirl #1   Whatever.

Schoolgirl #2   Whatever, yeah, are you saying you can't tell them brothers apart now?

Liam   Yeah, like we all look the same though.

Schoolgirl #2   You're white, brov.

Liam   Yeah, nah nah . . . –

Schoolgirl #2   You're whiter than white.

Liam   Nah, yeah, I know that though.

Schoolgirl #1   Cilit Bang.

Schoolgirl #2   Cilit Bang!

Schoolgirl #1   Bare toilet cleaner, cuz.

Schoolgirl #2   Oh my days, like bleach though! –

Schoolgirl #1 *takes another photo of* **Liam**.

Liam   – Nah, bleach then, jokes.

Schoolgirl #2   Write that under there though init? Hashtag bleach.

Schoolgirl #1   Hashtag Ed Sheeran. – (*Sings.*) 'Keep me inside the pocket . . .'

Schoolgirl #1 and **#2** (*sing*)   '. . . of your ripped jeans, holding me closer!'

They laugh, as **Schoolgirl #2** *dumps her half-eaten box of chicken and chips under the shelter, and stands up, grabbing her bag.*

Liam   Yeah, nah, write it down . . . –

Schoolgirl #2 (*pulling* **Schoolgirl #1** *up by the arm*)   – Here, come man, the 322.

Liam   Ed Sheeran, cool.

Schoolgirl #2   Move your butt, Madison, I aint dealing with this bus.

Schoolgirl #1   Oh my days, you serious? . . . –

Schoolgirl #2 *pulls* **Schoolgirl #1** *off the bench and out the shelter, dragging her by the arm.*

Schoolgirl #1   Yo, watch my sleeve! Stop yanking at me, bitch, fuck!

Liam *remains standing close by for a few moments.*

He watches the **Schoolgirls** *go, hesitates, makes to follow them, when . . .*

Liam *notices that the* **Third Older Schoolgirl** *is watching him.*

Liam   Nah, cool then, fourteen . . . –

Third Older Schoolgirl *also puts her phone's headphones in her ears, continuing to read her book.*

Liam   Fourteen, fifteen or whatever.

Pause.

Liam   Yeah.

Liam *moves to and makes to sit on the end of the bench.*

Liam   Yeah, so like just reading then or . . . –

A **Woman with a Pushchair** *(and baby) enters, moving to the bench, and . . .*

Liam *immediately makes room for her, standing up and returning to his original corner of the shelter.*

Liam   Nah nah, 'course.

The **Woman with a Pushchair** *busies herself, straightening the pushchair and the baby's clothes.*

Pause.

Liam   Busy?

Pause.

Liam   You busy then init?

Pause.

Liam   Taking care of her.

Pause.

Liam   Taking care of the little one then.

Beat.

Liam   Yeah, you're like sort of . . . –

Third Older Schoolgirl   She's busy, mate, yeah.

The **Third Schoolgirl** *keeps reading, and the* **Woman with a Pushchair** *attends to her baby, while both keep one eye on their phones and begin to tap/scroll.*

Liam *sees the discarded chicken box and pushes it further under the bench with his foot.*

Long pause.

Liam *moves out of the shelter, and to the bus sign post.*

He looks at the numbers, looks up the road.

Pause.

Liam *hesitates, then exits.*

The **Teenage Boy***, who is still leant on the hoarding, smoking his joint, watches him go.*

7.

Roadworks.

A section of pavement and road that is cordoned off with tape and cones and signs.

The pavement/road has been dug up, new pipes are being laid.

Three **Builders***, a short distance away from* **Liam** *as he quickly enters. The first two* **Builders** *are having a break, smoking and talking.* **Builder #1** *(Polish) is resting (just) on a cone,* **Builder #2** *is standing next to him, holding his phone in one hand and goggles in another. They are both smoking. They are sharing a joke and chuckling as the scene begins.*

Builder #1 (*in Polish*) . . . – like this, standing just like this. Meowing, holding one paw up? And then if I just leave her there, she starts tearing up the rug. Here, look . . . –

They continue chuckling as **Builder #1** *shows his colleague a picture on his phone.*

Pause.

Builder #1 (*in Polish*) Fuck, man, that cat is like Robert Mugabe.

Builder #2 *scrolls through the pictures.*

Builder #1 (*in Polish*) You leave home, your family, you go through hell to find work. And all you've got to show for it is the cat. She's beautiful though, hm?

The third **Builder** *is bent over, picking up lengths of orange piping, and carrying them from one end of the site to the other.*

When **Liam** *enters, he is immediately blocked by the roadworks.*

Pause.

He kicks one of the cones, but it doesn't fall.

Pause.

Liam *goes to move the cone to make his way through, when . . .*

The third **Builder** *has arrived by* **Liam**'s *end of the roadworks, holding a length of orange piping.*

Liam Keeping busy though init?

The third **Builder** *aggressively throws the piping to the ground, and walks back the way he came.*

Pause.

Liam *moves and bends down, and tidies up the bits of piping.*

Pause.

He tidies up another bit of piping, straightening it next to the first, when . . .

The third **Builder** *turns and gives him a dirty look.*

Liam *quickly exits the way he came.*

8.

The bus stop (same as before).

There is no one in the shelter.

Schoolgirl #2's discarded chicken box is still on the floor by the bench.

The **Teenage Boy** *has moved to the other side of the shelter, leant on the advertising hoarding. He smokes another small joint, and is texting on his phone.*

Liam, *bag over his shoulder, quickly enters. (He doesn't see the* **Teenage Boy**.*)*

He moves into the shelter and sits on the bench, checking his surroundings.

Long pause.

Liam *nudges the discarded chicken box with his foot.*

Pause.

He leans down and picks it up.

He opens the box and peers inside.

Pause.

Liam *rummages inside the box and begins wolfing down the leftovers (mainly fries).*

Pause.

Liam *nearly wretches.*

Pause.

He gets his breath back and starts eating the leftovers again, as . . .

The **Teenage Boy**, *having spotted* **Liam**, *sidles round and stands by the edge of the shelter, joint in hand.*

Long pause.

Teenage Boy So long time.

Pause. **Liam** *shuts the chicken box, attempts to hide it.*

Teenage Boy Liam . . . –

Liam Yeah, long-time.

Teenage Boy Not seen you in long time.

Liam Yeah man, time.

Teenage Boy Should try up the Foodbank init?

Liam Oh . . . –

Teenage Boy That shit is narsty, brov.

Liam Nah nah, just . . . –

Liam *slips the chicken box into his rucksack.*

Liam Find a bin or something, cool.

Teenage Boy So you still see Lamari and them boys?

Liam Nah, yeah yeah . . . –

Teenage Boy I aint seen no one, brov, no one.

The **Teenage Boy** *moves and sits on the bench next to* **Liam**, *who zips up his bag.*

Teenage Boy *offers* **Liam** *his joint.*

Liam Nah nah, I'm . . . –

Teenage Boy You sure, fam?

Liam Yeah, nah, I'm sure I'm sure.

Liam *stands up, pulls his bag over his shoulder.*

He makes to leave.

Teenage Boy   Well, if you ever want some t'ing.

Liam   Yeah? – Oh, what like . . . ?

Teenage Boy   Some t'ing, brov, init, look.

Teenage Boy *shows* **Liam** *the contents of his pockets.*

Liam   Ah, fuck.

Teenage Boy   Anything you want, G, check it.

Liam   Yeah, nah . . . – Like anything then?

Teenage Boy   Doing like plenty business.

Liam   Nah, wicked, so like . . . ? –

Teenage Boy   Anything you want. Lamari or Jamal or anyone. Some little . . . –

A melodic message alert on the **Teenage Boy**'s *phone.*

He checks the message.

Teenage Boy (*as he does so*)   Little blunt or something.

Liam   Thanks, nah, anything.

Teenage Boy *puts his phone away.*

Teenage Boy (*as he does so*)   You come and find me then. Tell them boys.

Teenage Boy *offers* **Liam** *his hand,* **Liam** *shakes it.*

Teenage Boy   Long time.

Liam   Long time init.

Teenage Boy (*still shaking* **Liam**'s *hand, not turning round*)   Toyota on the corner.

Liam   Eh?

Teenage Boy   Black Toyota on the corner. You see it? Is it still there?

Liam *peers.*

Liam   Nah. Nah, not, no . . . –

The **Teenage Boy** *breaks away, sitting down on the bench.*

Liam   Alright, so laters then, wicked.

Teenage Boy   Cool, brov, laters.

Liam *quickly exits.*

Teenage Boy   Come check me though, yeah?

Liam *is away down the road, and enters . . .*

9.

. . . the balcony/walkway, bag over his shoulder.

The curtains on number 22 are shut.

Paula *is standing in the doorway of number 23.*

Paula   It's Stephen isn't it?

Liam (*approaches*)   Liam.

Paula   Liam, okay.

Paula *blocks* **Liam***'s way with her hand.*

Liam   Sorry, yeah, she said she'd tell you.

Paula   Okay.

Liam   Yeah, nah, in there before. Next door, I mean.
Blonde.

Paula   Oh yeah, she's blonde alright. Well travelled.

Liam   Right, yeah, 'cause she said he was in the park or
something?

Paula   Well, no he wasn't.

Liam Oh . . . –

Paula He wasn't anywhere near the park, I was in the park. I was letting the dogs have a run.

Liam Okay then, wicked.

Paula She told you that then did she? Don't know why she told you that.

Liam Shit, nah . . . –

Paula Shit, nah, tragic. Can't have her crystal ball with her today.

Liam Oh, right, nah . . . –

Paula What you looking for?

Liam What?

Pause.

Liam Okay, nah . . . – Sorry, I . . . –

Paula Well he's took the train into town, I'm afraid, Stephen. Him and his friends.

Liam Oh so town, yeah, course. Jamal and everyone.

Paula No, not Jamal, his real friends. Late-night shopping on Oxford Street or whatever it is they've decided to do. Sports Direct.

Liam Cool, yeah, I knew that. Sports Direct n'shit.

Paula No, not 'and shit'.

Liam What, sorry?

Paula You should try his mobile if you've got something to say. You tried ringing his mobile at all?

Liam He changed his number I think.

Paula Well, not lately he hasn't.

Liam   No, I can't call out I mean. I need a new top-up thing, the card?

Liam *takes his phone from his pocket, showing* **Paula**.

Liam   Like the card I think, see?

Paula   I'm not interested in your problems, Stephen, sorry. Did you need him for anything in particular?

Liam   Okay.

Paula   No, I asked a question. What did you want to see him for exactly?

Liam   Yeah, nah, next door.

Paula   Next door? You know she's about ten years too old for you with a toddler.

Liam   Ah right then, cool, so he's bussin'-up with Jamal and ting?

Paula   No, I told you, we don't see Jamal no more, I've already told you that. They're his friends from the community centre. Lamari's been keeping himself busy . . . –

Liam   Oh, them boys, right.

Paula   Them boys, yeah, the sort that keep themselves busy. Workshops, football with the youngsters, that sort of thing.

Liam   Nah, we all have.

Paula   What?

Liam   No, I have I mean. I've like been busy at the workshop. Football n'ting.

Paula   Right, and I suppose you'll be starting your A-levels soon?

Liam   Nah, yeah, A-levels.

Paula   When do you start on them then? Straight after Jeremy Kyle?

Liam   Nah, yeah, I don't know.

Paula   'Nah, yeah, I don't know.'

Liam   Nah, cool, sort of . . . –

Paula   Don't know much, Stephen, do you really? You know, there's some of us choose to work.

Liam   Oh, right . . . –

Paula   Some of us choose to work really fucking hard to get somewhere, Stephen, yeah.

You know Lamari's . . . –

Liam   Nah, Lamari, cool, he said.

Paula   What, sorry?

Liam   Nah, that's what he said. Lamari, I mean, he said that before.

Paula   He said what before? – (*Blocking* **Liam** *from entering the flat.*) Sorry, what are you doing?

Liam   Oh nah . . . –

Paula   I've told you, he's out. – What the hell you trying to creep past me for?

Liam   Nah, just . . . –

Paula   Stay there, right there.

Liam   Just Call of Duty I thought.

Paula   What?

Liam   Nah, Call of Duty, X-Box. What we usually do.

Paula   You don't usually do nothing.

Liam   Nah, okay . . . –

Paula   Not here you don't.

Liam   Okay then, sick.

Paula   Speak properly.

Liam   Oh . . . –

Paula   You come to my door, you speak properly, Stephen.

Liam   It's Liam.

Paula   What?

Liam   Not fucking Stephen, it's Liam.

Paula   Oh . . . –

Liam   Not fucking Stephen, it's Liam!

Pause.

Paula   Okay, Liam, you can leave now, please?

Liam   Oh, right . . . – What, so . . . ?

Paula   Yes. Step away from the door . . . –

Liam   Step away from the door then.

Paula   I've got my two dogs inside.

Liam   Who, sorry?

Paula   No, not 'who', the dogs.

Liam   Oh, right . . . – So, dogs then, yeah?

Paula *exits, shutting/bolting the door behind her.*

Long pause.

Liam *goes to knock at the door.*

Beat.

He doesn't.

Pause.

Liam *moves to the window of number 22.*

He bends over and tries, with difficulty, to peer in through the letterbox as a **Young Mum with Pushchair**, *with shopping bags hanging off the pushchair handles, enters.*

Liam *is blocking her way.*

Young Mum with Pushchair   Sorry, skuse?

Liam *doesn't move, and* **Young Mum with Pushchair** *gives him a nudge with the pushchair.*

Young Mum with Pushchair   Mind out, mate, you're . . . –

Liam *jumps, startled, and clumsily clatters past/over the pushchair.*

Young Mum with Pushchair   – Oi watch it, fucking hell! –

Liam *quickly exits down the walkway.*

Young Mum with Pushchair   – Watch what you're doing, you mong!

10.

Bus stop.

Early evening, getting dark.

A **Fashionable Foreign Student**, *chunky headphones resting round her neck, is peering at the bus timetable on the shelter. She also holds her iPhone, connected to the chunky headphones.*

Liam *quickly enters, bag over shoulder, and dumps himself on the empty bench.*

Long pause, as the **Foreign Student** *peers at her bus maps app on her iPhone, and then at the sign with the bus numbers.*

Foreign Student (*to* **Liam**)   West End, Oxford Street?

Pause.

The **Foreign Student** *checks/scrolls the app on her iPhone.*

Liam *watches her.*

Pause.

Foreign Student   Sorry. Sorry, excuse me . . . ?

*The **Foreign Student** moves over to **Liam**, displaying her iPhone travel app.*

Foreign Student   Do you know if I should get the train or change at Brixton for the underground?

Liam   Oh . . . –

Foreign Student   The 3 goes to Brixton?

Liam   Yeah, Brixton, 'course.

Foreign Student   I don't know, should I change there? I need Tottenham Court, Oxford Street.

Liam   Yeah, like Sports Direct.

Foreign Student (*looks on her app*)   Sports Direct? This says Piccadilly.

Liam   Oh, Piccadilly, seen. Like Piccadilly then, Oxford Street.

Foreign Student   Maybe the train would be better.

Liam   Nah, train then.

Foreign Student   West Norwood or Gipsy Hill?

Liam   Whichever, yeah, sort of . . .

Foreign Student   The overground at Crystal Palace I think.

Liam   Oh, is there? Wicked wicked . . . –

Foreign Student   You're not from round here?

Liam   Nah, 'course, I'm . . . Going into London n'ting.

Foreign Student   We are in London.

*The **Foreign Student** giggles at him, moves and returns to the bus shelter timetable.*

She peers at it.

Long pause.

The **Foreign Student** *makes a choice and exits.*

Pause.

Liam *gets up and moves to the bus shelter timetable.*

He peers at it.

Long pause.

Liam *goes to return to the bench.*

He stops, and hesitates.

Pause.

Liam *exits, in the same direction as the* **Foreign Student**.

11A.

On the train.

Evening.

On the tannoy we hear 'Southern, this is the Southern train to . . . London Victoria calling at Streatham Hill, Balham, Wandsworth Common, Clapham Junction, Battersea Park and London Victoria.'

The **Foreign Student**, *followed – a distance behind – by* **Liam**, *enters a carriage.*

The **Foreign Student** *finds a seat.*

Liam *finds an empty window seat on a four-seater section, a distance from the* **Foreign Student**.

He looks out of the window, still rubbing his leg where he was hit by the pushchair.

Pause.

On the adjacent seat, is an **Exhausted Middle-Aged Man** *in a security unifom, holding a folded-up newspaper (on the crossword page) and pen. He has his feet up on the seat opposite him, and is trying to stay awake, but staring directly at* **Liam**.

Pause.

Liam *avoids his gaze, as the* **Exhausted Middle-Aged Man** *then wipes his forehead with a tissue from his pocket.*

Pause.

Liam *leans back in his seat and also puts his feet up on the seat in front of him, dumping his bag on the seat next to him.*

11B.

On the train.

A stop or two later.

The tannoy can still be heard announcing stops.

The train is much busier now – various **Commuters** *peppered/ squeezed along the carriage.*

Liam *and the* **Exhausted Middle-Aged Man** *remain in the same seats.*

The **Exhausted Middle-Aged Man** *has his eyes closed, whether he is asleep or not.*

Sitting on a four-seater, with **Liam**, *are three drunk friends – two male –* **Andy** *and* **Dan** *one female,* **Nat**, *in her thirties.*

Sitting behind them on a single seat, on his own, is a man in a suit reading a paper, trying his best to ignore the noise the others are making.

Standing close by is a **Professional Man** *in his fifties, scrolling/ texting on his phone.*

The scene begins immediately with **Dan**'s *singing, and* **Nat** *and* **Andy**'s *chatting.*

A.

*The three drunk friends – **Andy**, **Nat** and **Dan** – are singing/chatting loudly on the four-seater, drinking bottles of lager and Bacardi.*

Dan *is very drunk, watching, and singing along to a Katy Perry video of 'Roar' on his phone, as **Andy** and **Nat** chatter.*

Nat – . . . can't bloody well believe they get away with charging that.

Andy Yeah well it's because they know they're selling to addicts don't they? Get away with murder, I remember when it was under five pounds for a packet of twenty, robbing bastards.

Nat How much do you spend a week then? Must cost you a bit mustn't it?

B.

C.

*The **Professional Man** in his fifties answers his phone and speaks for the duration of the scene. At some point, following the entrance of the **Young Muslim Man**,* *he may move from his seat and exit to another carriage, but he stays talking on the phone.*

Professional Man (*on the phone*)   – Yeah, nearly . . . – Nearly, yeah, a couple of minutes probably . . . –

No, I don't know, Chinese? . . . – Chinese, yeah, what do you fancy? . . . –

Go onto Hungry House. – . . . Hungry House, it'll ask for my password . . . –

A few moments later, a **Homeless Guy** *enters the carriage on the furthest end away from* **Liam.**

Andy   Oh, fuck knows. Forty quid, I dunno, fifty . . .

Nat   Fifty quid?! Fucking hell, you're joking! How do you manage that then?

Andy   I don't, that's the point, why do you think I'm always owing out to everyone else? Paying for tonight on this dodgy Aqua card 'cause I've overdrawn everywhere else.

Nat   Oh shut up, no you aint.

Andy   I fucking am.

Nat   You should think about giving up I think.

Andy   I don't want to give up, I like it. It's about the only thing I've got to look forward to most days. That, and a night out with you cunts every two years, rest of it's bullshit, the fuck do I care?

Nat 'Them Vapour things, the funnels.

Andy Oh give me strength Vapour, can you see me with one of them? – 'Ere, come on, Dan, you shit-bollock, give it a rest!

Nat Got to pace it, mate, still got the whole night ahead of us.

Andy The fuck has he ever paced shit?

Nat Don't want to peak too early, I'll slit my wrists if I'm home before Jamie's gone to bed. I've left him watching /War and Peace on iPlayer.

Dan (*sings*) – /and you're gonna hear me . . . –

Dan/Andy – . . . roar'!!

He stands, facing the other passengers, and makes his announcement . . .

Homeless Guy Good evening ladies and gentleman, sorry to disturb you, I promise I won't take up too much of your time. As you can probably see, I'm currently homeless, I've been sleeping rough for the last five nights because I couldn't afford a hostel. I would, of course, be very grateful . . . –

He is drowned out by the singing from **Andy** *and* **Nat** *for a moment.*

No, it's got a thing, auto-fill, auto-correct or whatever . . . – It should just come up for you, yeah, go onto Great Wall. –

. . . Great Wall, it's one of the first that appears . . . – Five stars . . . – Four and a half, five . . . –

Well, there's a box that asks you for Cuisine. – . . . No, I know I didn't, but . . . – Cuisine, yeah, put in Chinese . . . – Alright, yeah, I will. . . . .

Nat   /Christ, I hate that song.

Andy   Oh fuck off, it's classic. Classiiiic!.

Nat   You're going to get us thrown off I think.

Andy   Can't beat a bit of Katy. Like a blow-up doll aint she? Looks exactly like a sex toy. –

Nat   Yeah, and you'd know.

Andy   Well I know there's not a man in the world would throw her out of bed. Tits like that, they're her USB.

Nat   What?

Andy   Her USB, you know. What they use to sell this garbage.

Nat   That's USP, you nutter.

Homeless Guy   Be very grateful if you could find it in your hearts to donate any food or spare bits of change so that I can try and get myself a bed for the night. Anything you can contribute – anything at all – will indeed go a very long way.

*The **Homeless Guy** takes a moment to straighten himself, pick his bag up, and takes a small plastic cup from his pocket.*

He walks through the carriage.

– It's in my hand, yeah. . . . – Yeah, just text me or something. . . . – Let me know. . . – No, I do . . . – I'm totally in the mood, yeah . . . – Great Wall, it's in . . . . – It's in Forest Hill I think . . . –

Okay then, ribs . . . – Spare ribs, yeah . . . – Barbecue spare ribs, egg fried rice . . . – Some of those pork balls. . . . – Pork balls. – No, the things, the . . . – The round pork balls, yeah. . . Nah, alright. . . . – Alright, yeah, starving, yeah. –

Andy Yeah, that's what I said, Nat, fuck off . . . –

Nat USB! You heard this?

Andy All about the sales, the marketing. She wouldn't even have a career if she didn't carry on like a slut.

Nat Oi, don't say that, I fucking hate that word.

Andy Yeah yeah, the equality police again.

Nat No, I just don't like that word.

Andy Nothing like a bit of empty feminism to get you in the mood. – (*Sings to the video.*) Oh oh oh oh oh oh!

Nat Oh my god, Andy . . . –

The **Exhausted Middle-Aged Man** *reaches into his pocket and plops a coin into the* **Homeless Guy***'s cup as he passes.*

Homeless Guy Bless you, sir, thanks.

. . . I don't know, a toastie . . . – Can't even remember, just a toastie or something, yeah . . . Nothing remarkable. . . . – No, I just couldn't . . . I couldn't be bothered at the time, it's not important. . . – Well, I am now. . . . – Yeah. . . . Yeah, they'll send you a notification. . . . An email. They're meant to send you an email, a notification. . . . – Check your spam if it doesn't, it should say Hungry House? . . . – Receipt of order, receipt . . . – A receipt, a confirmation with the time. . . . –

Andy *grabs the phone off* **Dan** *and puts it on his groin, gyrating as he sings.*

Andy (*sings, gyrates, laughs*)   Oh oh oh oh oh oh oh . . . –

The **Homeless Guy** *fingers the coin out of the cup and puts it in his pocket, passing down the carriage.*

Nat   You're not impressing anyone, you know that? 'Ere . . . –

Nat grabs the phone from **Andy**, *and presses buttons.*

He reaches the end of the carriage occupied by the **Professional Man** *in his fifties, who is talking on his phone.*

Nat   Put something else on now, fucking carriage full of people.

Homeless Guy (*to the* **Professional Man**)   Good to see there's some humanity left in the world, eh?

The **Homeless Guy** *squeezes past them, holding out his plastic cup.*

Andy   – Oi, watch your shit there, fella, eh?

Nat (*under her breath, to* **Andy**)   Oh Jesus Christ, that's gross . . . –

Yeah, well that's probably the same thing, ignore me. -. . . – Ignore me, yes, that's your best bet, bye.

Andy 'Course he's gross, that's his USB.

Nat (*under her breath, to* **Andy**) Honestly, I think I might actually be sick? Where are we now, Balham?

Liam (*chipping in*) It's Balham, yeah.

Nat Might have to move to another carriage I think.

Andy Don't be stupid, it's like being out in the countryside. Just got to train your nostrils. – 'Ere . . .

Liam Balham, look.

Andy Change the music, take your mind off it.

Liam It's Balham, cuz, the sign.

The **Professional Man in His 50's** *moves down the carriage away from him.*

A **Young Muslim Man** *enters the carriage.*

Andy   Yeah, thanks mate, good of you. – 'Ere, pick something decent, Nat, something for everyone.

Nat   Give me a minute, thing won't let me do anything, the screen's all wet.

A few moments later, when the **Young Muslim Man** *has entered, standing close by . . .*

Andy   Nice bag, mate!

Nat   Sssshhh. Fucking hell, Andy, don't . . . –

Andy   What is that, Berghaus? Was thinking of getting one myself. 'Ere, mate!

Nat   Oh my god, shut up . . . –

Andy   Should get down Stamford Bridge, do us all a favour. – (*To* **Nat.**) – What? He knows

Homeless Guy (*to the Young Muslim Man*) – Nice to feel welcome, isn't it mate?

I'm only joking, you don't have to pull that face.

Nat I'm not pulling a fucking face.

Andy So how come you look like you just swallowed a lemon then, you got the shits? –

Nat selects a music video on the phone – Jay Z's 'Empire State of Mind'.

Andy – Oh tune!

12.

The barriers by the main concourse.

Evening.

It is very busy. Lots of **Commuters***, passing through the barriers – touching in (or out) with their Oyster cards. Sounds of the station.*

A **Uniformed Man** *and a* **Uniformed Lady***.*

The **Uniformed Man** *has a handset/walkie-talkie device that he keeps close to his ear.*

He is chewing gum incessantly.

The **Uniformed Lady** *addresses* **Liam** *and the* **Homeless Guy** *at the gated barrier, blocking their way through.*

Uniformed Lady   Oyster card.

Homeless Guy   Yeah, he's got mine, darling, no worries.

Liam   What?

Homeless Guy   Do the thing for me, mate, won't you? Touch in touch out or whatever . . . –

The **Homeless Guy** *ducks behind* **Liam** *and races through the barrier, barging/pushing past the other* **Commuters***.*

Uniformed Lady   You've got your card with you?

Liam   Yeah, 'course. Nah, like I was about to . . . –

Liam *tries to walk through the barriers, following the* **Homeless Guy***, but the* **Uniformed Lady** *blocks his way.*

Uniformed Lady   You don't get through without it. – (*Calls.*) Asif!

Liam   Yeah, but . . . –

Uniformed Lady   Never mind your friend, you need to touch in.

The **Uniformed Lady** *signals to the* **Uniformed Man**, *who exits through the barriers in the* **Homeless Guy**'s *direction.*

Liam   Oh . . . –

Uniformed Lady   Show me your card please, have you got it?

Liam   Oh, got it? Nah, yeah, I got it, I got it . . . –

Liam *rummages in his pockets.*

Liam   Sort of thing I think. – Sorry, he just . . . –

Uniformed Lady   He just what, sorry?

Liam   Before, I mean. On the train . . . –

Uniformed Lady   You were on that train? So where did you travel from?

Liam   Nah, I dunno . . . –

Uniformed Lady   Where did you get on?

Liam   West Norwood I think.

Uniformed Lady   Right, and you know it's a twenty-pound penalty if you don't have a valid ticket? You understand that?

Liam   Cool then, twenty pound.

Uniformed Lady   And up to two thousand pounds if we prove wilful intent.

Liam   Wilful what, sorry? – Nah, 'cause the bus only went to Brixton? Sports Direct.

Uniformed Lady   Alright . . . –

Liam   Sports Direct, Oxford Street.

Uniformed Lady   Well, you're miles away from Oxford Street.

Liam   Oh, is it?

Uniformed Lady   Alright, well if you can purchase a ticket with my colleague over there? –

At this point, the **Uniformed Man** *re-enters, manning the barriers.*

Liam   – So like this isn't where I thought then?

Uniformed Lady   Victoria Station, that's the Victoria train. How much have you got on you?

Liam   I don't know, bits.

Uniformed Lady   Bits?

Liam   Bits, yeah. And I can't just like . . . ?

Uniformed Lady   Once you've got a valid ticket.

Liam   – Nah, fuck, sorry . . .

Uniformed Lady   How much have you got on you exactly, can I see?

Liam   Okay then, okay. Fuck . . . —

Uniformed Lady   It's four pound twenty a single journey, and if you . . . -.

Liam *pushes past the* **Professional Man** *in his fifties – from the train – knocking him into the* **Uniformed Lady**, *and runs.*

Professional Man   – Ow, Jesus . . . !

Uniformed Lady   My apologies, sir, / are you okay? – Asif!

Professional Man   – No I'm not okay, some of us pay our fares.

Liam *races out through the barriers, barging past* **Commuters** *as he is pursued by the* **Uniformed Man**.

13.

Victoria Overground Station.

Evening.

Noise and lights.

A constant stream of people – commuters, theatre-goers, revellers, homeless – pass by or stand in the station's outside concourse smoking, talking, waiting for their trains.

By the main entrance of the station, outside, **Liam** *is cornered by two* **Police Officers**.

The **Professional Man** *in his fifties stands with them, and a* **Homeless Teenage Girl** *is sitting on the floor in a sleeping bag, also watching, and guarding her belongings from getting trampled on.*

Liam Ah, shit, sorry . . . –

Police Officer #1 Stand here for me, please?

Liam Sorry, yeah, you're right. Just here then . . .

Professional Man You know you needn't be so bloody rough with him.

Police Officer #1 No one's being rough. –

Professional Man I'd call it rough.

Police Officer #1 – Alright, just stand up against the wall for me, please.

Liam What, you mean like . . . ? – Cool, yeah.

Homeless Teenager Hey watch you're dragging your shoes man, look where you're going!

Liam Oh, really? Nah . . .

Homeless Teenager All over my shit, man, fuck.

Police Officer #1 Then why don't you move on, Ruby?

Homeless Teenager You move, wanker, I was here first . . . –

Police Officer #1 We're on a public concourse, you know that.

Homeless Teenager Kick my flipping drink everywhere.

Liam Sorry, I couldn't see . . . –

Homeless Teenager The fuck you couldn't see.

Police Officer #1 What's your name?

Professional Man How about I pay his fare? I'm not sure you need to . . . –

Police Officer #1 Alright, thank you.

Professional Man – . . . go to these lengths, it's only a train ticket, he didn't actually hurt me particularly.

Police Officer #1 Your name?

Liam Yeah, Stephen, yeah. Liam, I mean.

Professional Man Liam, yeah, let me lend you a fiver. – (*To* **Police Officer #1**.) Will a fiver do it you think?

Homeless Teenager Depends what you're after.

Police Officer #1 (*to* **Professional Man**)   Sir, please, I appreciate you're trying to help . . . –

Professional Man It's not a big deal really.

Police Officer #1 Well we'll determine that, that's why we're here.

Professional Man He's just a kid, look.

Police Officer #1 Thank you, yep.

Homeless Teenager Yeah, fuck off fatty, try your luck down the gents.

Police Officer #1 Mind if we look inside your bag do you, Liam?

Liam I don't know, yeah . . . –

Police Officer #2 *takes* **Liam**'s *bag and searches through it.*

Police Officer #1 Anything we should know about?

Liam Whatever, cool. Whatever you say, sir . . . –

Liam *accidentally steps on* **Homeless Girl**'*s sleeping bag, knocking her drink.*

Homeless Teenager   – Oi, fuck! Fuck, man, that's not right!

Police Officer #1   Alright . . . –

Homeless Teenager   Regular latte, two pounds sixty . . . –

Professional Man   Regular latte?

Homeless Teenager   Why shouldn't I have a flipping latte?

Police Officer #2 *manipulates* **Liam**'*s arms for him, as* **Police Officer #1** *frisks and searches* **Liam**'*s pockets.*

Police Officer #1   – And how old are you?

Liam   Nah, seventeen.

Police Officer #1   Seventeen?

Liam   Yeah . . . –

Homeless Teenager   Take him across Dolphin Square to show your mates.

Police Officer #1   You should keep your voice down. – (*To* **Liam**.) Do you mind if we call your parents, Liam? Check you're who you say you are.

Liam   Check, yeah, 'course 'course . . . –

Police Officer #1   Mind if we call them, you want to give me their number? – (*To* **Professional Man**.) Move along now, thank you. – (*To* **Liam**.) Unless you want to come with us to the station?

Liam   Oh . . .

Homeless Teenager   You can flipping well take me if you've got a cell going, mate.

Police Officer #1   You can find your own bed, Ruby, we're not falling for that again. – (*To* **Liam**.) If you'd rather we sort this out at the station?

Liam   Nah, Oxford Street I think.

Police Officer #1   Where?

Liam   Me and my friends, like if you tell me the way? If I can like pay you back? Like if you let the man pay or something? What he said.

Professional Man   Look, it's my mistake really. Perhaps if you just let me go to the machines and get him a ticket . . . –

Police Officer #1   No, that won't be necessary.

Professional Man   But surely if it saves you the paperwork . . . –

Homeless Teenager   Let him do his job, man, stay away off my shit.

Police Officer #1   Your parents be home will they, ?

Liam   Fuck, no, I dunno . . . Could be.

Police Officer #1   You got a landline?

Liam   At work somewhere I think.

Police Officer #1   What?

Liam   Nah, they're at work all the time, I dunno, like I don't have any credit? My thing, my phone, the battery on the thing.

Police Officer #1 (*hands him his bag*)   Alright, Liam, calm down . . . – Consider this a warning, alright? Get going, move along.

Liam   Where, sorry?

Police Officer #1   Wherever it is you're going, Liam, go on.

14A.

Victoria Station public toilets.

Toilet cubicle.

Liam *quickly enters and sits on the toilet, and removes his bag from his shoulder.*

He rummages around and takes out the Morley's chicken box.

He opens it and takes a few bites from the remains.

Chews and swallows.

Pause.

Liam *eats every last scrap of food from the chicken box.*

Long pause.

He looks for toilet paper to wipe his mouth.

There isn't any, so he wipes his mouth with his sleeve.

He dumps the chicken box on the floor and kicks it out of the cubicle, as . . .

A **Toilet Attendant***, holding a mop and bucket, stops outside the cubicle and surveys the chicken box.*

Toilet Attendant   Pick up your litter when you've done. Hello?

14B.

The Mall, close by Buckingham Palace.

Night.

Liam*, bag over his shoulder, walks in one direction.*

Long pause.

He stops, turns, walks in another direction.

14C.

Edgware Road.

Night.

Liam, *bag over his shoulder, walks in one direction.*

He crosses a road.

He walks in another direction.

15.

Oxford Street, Sports Direct store.

Around midnight.

The Sports Direct store-front is open and illuminated, but the shutters are about to come down.

A **Sports Direct Security Guard**, *in Sports Direct shirt and trousers, holding a walkie-talkie, is standing in the entrance.*

Liam *enters, bag over shoulder.*

He stops by the front of the Sports Direct store, attempting to peer in.

Pause.

Sports Direct Security Guard   We're closed for the night.

Liam   Nah fuck off you aint.

Sports Direct Security Guard   What?

Liam   Nah, just . . . The light on inside, sorry.

Sports Direct Security Guard   Yeah, and we're shutting up, look.

Liam   Can I see inside?

Sports Direct Security Guard   The store is closed.

Liam   Them people in there, there's like someone still there I think?

Sports Direct Security Guard   Yeah, because we're clearing up.

Liam   Late-night shopping though.

Sports Direct Security Guard   We're busy, go home.

Liam *steps back as the shutters come down, and the* **Security Guard** *vanishes behind them.*

Pause.

Liam *peers through the shutters.*

Long pause.

Liam *leans on the building.*

Long pause.

Liam *walks on, exits.*

16.

Outside a nightclub.

West End/Soho.

1.00 or 2.00 am.

Sounds of loud, banging music coming from inside the club.

The doorway to the nightclub, with a **Bouncer** *tapping and scrolling on his phone.*

A **Young Woman** *and* **Young Man** *(early twenties) are sprawled, unconscious, by the fire exit doorway, a short distance from the main entrance. They are both wasted from booze, half-asleep.*

He wears a t-shirt and skinny jeans and has been sick. He is slumped on the edge of the doorway.

There is puke on the ground close by.

She wears sunglasses, a very short skirt, crop-top and a leather jacket hanging off her shoulders.

She is sitting on the fire exit floor with him, resting on his back.

There may also be some drunk or drugged-up passers-by, leaving or entering the club.

Liam *enters, bag over shoulder.*

He stops by the entrance of the nightclub, trying to peer in.

The **Bouncer** *looks up from his phone.*

He takes one look at **Liam**, *snorts, then returns to his phone.*

Liam *backs away from the entrance, and stands closer to the young couple, still trying to peer into the nightclub, but avoiding the* **Bouncer**.

Long pause.

Young Woman   You got any drugs?

Pause.

Young Woman   Hello, excuse me?

The **Young Woman** *leans across and tries tapping* **Liam** *on his leg.*

Young Woman   Have you got any drugs?

Pause.

Young Woman   Any drugs, anything at all.

Liam *shakes his head.*

Long pause.

The **Young Woman** *taps* **Liam** *on the leg.*

Young Woman   Olivia.

The **Young Woman** *offers* **Liam** *her hand.*

Young Woman   Olivia, Livvy.

Liam *reaches down and shakes her hand.*

Liam   Liam.

Young Woman   Hello, Liam, something to keep me up.

Beat.

Young Woman   Something to keep me up, I'm fucked.

The **Young Woman** *rests back down on her boyfriend's back.*

Long pause.

The **Young Woman** *rises again, and taps* **Liam** *on the shoulder.*

Young Woman   I'll give you a blowjob.

Pause.

Young Woman   You look like you sell them, you look really dodgy.

Pause.

Young Woman   Get me some drugs and I'll suck your dick.

Beat.

Young Woman   Oh, don't worry about him, he shits himself around normal people.

The **Young Man** *starts to retch or pukes.*

The **Young Woman** *sits up, tapping the* **Young Man** *on his back.*

Young Woman   I bet you've got a knife haven't you?

Pause.

Young Woman   Do you carry it around with you then?

Liam   Nah, I don't know, sometimes.

Young Woman   That's cool.

Pause.

Young Woman   I said that's cool, that's awesome.

Liam   Thanks, yeah. Awesome.

Young Woman   Yeah, I think I'm a bit scared of you
actually.

Pause.

Young Woman   I'm a bit scared of you I think, yeah. In a
good way.

Liam   Nah, yeah . . . –

The **Young Man** *pukes.*

Pause.

Young Woman   I'm really fucked, sorry.

Liam   Nah, that's good then init? Plenty business. Anything
you want, cuz.

The **Young Woman** *has passed out again.*

Pause.

Liam *reaches over and strokes the* **Young Woman***'s hair.*

Pause.

The **Bouncer** *is watching* **Liam***.*

Liam *stops.*

He exits one way.

Long pause.

Liam *re-enters, makes for the club entrance . . .*

The **Bouncer** *looks up from his phone, and* **Liam** *exits the
other way.*

17.

The third floor walkway/balcony.

6.00 a.m.

Early-morning light, some early-morning sounds.

Liam *is slumped down on the ground. He's been there a long time.*

Long pause.

The door of number 23 opens, and **Lamari** *enters.*

He wears a smart tracksuit and carries a bag of footballs over his shoulder, as **Liam** *jumps to his feet and moves across to him.*

Liam (*as he does so*)   So you're keeping busy then, yo.

Liam *sticks out his fist for a fist bump.* **Lamari** *doesn't respond.*

Beat.

Liam   Like you're busy then init? Football n'ting, Sports Direct.

Lamari   The fuck you doing here, Gollum?

Liam   Nah, just . . . –

Lamari   You looking for your precious then still? The fuck you creeping round my door at six in the morning?

Liam   Oh, what . . . ?

Lamari   'Oh, what? Oh, what?' The fuck you doing creeping around? School's over, brov, slide, I don't need you stinking out my yard.

Liam   Stinking out, cuz, funny. Nah, 'cause I was late.

Lamari   What?- I swear to god, you look like some sort of tramp then, Gollum.

Liam   Long walk back.

Lamari   What?

Liam   Long walk back though init?

Liam *holds out his fist for a fist bump again.*

Liam   Like long time, cuz.

Lamari   Say the thing.

Liam   The thing?

Lamari   The thing, bruv, say it.

Beat.

Lamari   The thing, Gollum, come.

Lamari *hits* **Liam** *on the arm.*

Liam   Nah, precious.

Lamari   Precious what?

Lamari *hits* **Liam** *on the arm.*

Lamari   Precious what?

Liam   Precious Baggins, yeah, my precious.

Lamari   So why do you let me do that to you, brov?

Liam   Nah, I don't know, sorry.

Lamari   School's over, Liam. Time to grow the fuck up.

Lamari *exits down the walkway.*

Long pause.

Liam *puts his bag over his shoulder and exits down the walkway.*

18.

Bedroom.

Morning.

Bunkbeds, posters on the walls of cute baby animals and Disney princesses.

Abandoned clothes and toys.

A pink portable television on top of the chest of drawers.

Liam *quickly enters, bag over shoulder.*

He shuts the door behind him.

He moves to the bottom bunk and sits, dropping the bag.

Pause.

Liam *collapses/lies back on the bed.*

Long pause.

Liam *sits up.*

He picks up the television remote control.

He switches it on – 'Peppa Pig' is on the television, the volume turned up high.

Liam *watches 'Peppa Pig'.*

Very long pause.

Liam *picks up the remote control and flicks channels.*

He finds a music video – Nicki Minaj – 'Anaconda' (or something like that) – bumping and grinding.

A few seconds, then . . .

Liam *flicks channels.*

A news channel.

Then, **Liam** *flicks channels.*

He finds 'Peppa Pig'.

He watches.

Then turns the television off.

Long pause.

Liam *moves to the bedroom door.*

On a hook on the door is a tatty school rucksack.

He takes the rucksack off the hook and opens it.

Rummaging inside, **Liam** *removes his old school uniform – blazer, shirt and tie.*

He looks at them.

Pause.

Liam *undresses, taking his t-shirt and hoodie/trackie top off.*

He stuffs these in the rucksack.

Pause.

Liam *puts on the shirt and blazer.*

Pause.

He reaches in the blazer pocket and removes his school tie.

Pause.

Liam *moves to and stands in front of the mirror – also, on the back of the bedroom door.*

He puts on his school tie.

He doesn't do it very well.

Pause.

Liam *picks up the rucksack and fits it over his shoulder.*

He undoes his school tie.

He reties his school tie.

19.

The Jobcentre.

Day.

Liam *sits at a desk, opposite a suited Client Advisor,* **Lloyd**.

There is a PC on the desk.

It is mid-meeting.

Lloyd *is tap-tapping on the PC.*

Lloyd   You thought about college?

Beat.

Lloyd   College, night school, that sort of thing.

Liam   Oh . . . –

Lloyd   Technical academy.

Liam   Yeah, cool.

Lloyd   Yeah? Some sort of course then maybe?

Liam   Nah like I might I think.

Lloyd *gives* **Liam** *a look.*

Liam   Nah, yeah.

Lloyd   The get-up, the tie.

Liam   Oh, is it?

Lloyd   Might want to reconsider that, Liam.

Liam   Yeah, no.

Lloyd   I mean, I respect the intention, but . . . –

Liam   Respect, nah.

Lloyd   Probably not going to do you many favours if I'm honest. You should think about Youth Connections.

Liam   Okay, yeah, 'course.

Lloyd   Few mornings a week. They'll help you put a cv together, get some incentive.

Liam   Incentive, cool.

Lloyd   Then maybe think about doing some voluntary work. That sort of thing interest you?

Liam   Nah, yeah.

Lloyd   Something practical. Keep you busy at least, get some skills.

Liam   So like then skills then, you think?

Lloyd   Probably something like that I think, Liam, yeah. The thing is we can't actually put you in our system till you turn eighteen.

Liam   Nah, right, yeah, that's . . . –

Lloyd   That's just the law.

Liam   Wicked then.

Lloyd   What?

Liam   Not yet then, no?

Lloyd   Well there's nothing stopping you from looking in the meantime. You got a computer at home?

Liam   Yeah, nah . . . –

Lloyd   You've got a computer, you can go online. Have a look.

Liam   Yeah, nah . . . – Nah, like go online then, busy. Like if I can just keep busy? If I can have something . . .

Beat.

Liam   In the day.

Lloyd   What, sorry?

Liam   Nah, like in the meantime, in the day? What you said.

Lloyd   Well, you're welcome to use the machines down the front here. Or you could go to your local library maybe?

Liam   Local library.

Lloyd   They have computers you can use.

Client Advisor #2 (*arriving at his/her desk*)   Yeah, if he can find one open anywhere.

Liam   Nah, I can do that.

Lloyd   Might even get some reading done, Liam. Tell me, when do you turn eighteen?

Liam   Oh . . . – Oh, so what you mean like next year?

Lloyd   Next year?

Liam   Nah, like this time next year sort of thing. Eighteen n'shit.

Lloyd   Right, well there's not much we can do until then, Liam, I'm afraid.

Liam   Oh . . . –

Lloyd   Come back in eleven, twelve months' time, see what we can do then.

Liam   Nah, cool, alright.

Lloyd   Alright then, so . . . –

Liam   So come back sort of then then, init? Like next year?

Lloyd *offers* **Liam** *his hand – at which point* **Client Advisor #2** *gestures to* **Claimant #2** *and their dialogue begins at the third table.*

Beat.

Liam   Yeah, nah, thanks. Like in a year then.

Liam *takes* **Lloyd***'s hand and shakes.*

Lloyd *returns to his paperwork, computer, etc.*

Pause.

Liam *hesitates, then gets up, and makes to leave.*

As he passes through the Jobcentre, **Liam** *passes by three separate desks with three* **Claimants** *and three* **Client Advisors***, along with a number of* **Claimants** *waiting patiently/impatiently to be seen – tapping on phones, looking through their jobseekers' booklets, etc.*

A.

Client Advisor #1 *and*
Claimant #1 *are in mid-meeting.*

Claimant #1   – . . . he's five
years old, you can't expect me
to just leave him there.

Client Advisor #1   – And
you've had all the time in the
world for you to arrange your
child-care. This isn't a drop-in
centre, you can't just expect
. . . –

Claimant #1   And how do I
afford child-care when you put
me on a sanction?

Client Advisor #1   Well, if
you want to avoid being

B.

C.

Client Advisor #3 *is in mid-
meeting with* **Claimant #3.**

Client Advisor #3   No no, I
understand it's quite confusing,
I confuse myself sometimes.
The point is you applied for
PIP, the Personal
Independence Payment . . . –

Claimant #3   I know what
PIP is.

Client Advisor #3   Yes, and
your health assessment rules
that you were fit for work,
which is why I'm asking you
why you didn't show up for
your job interview.

sanctioned then you need to make sure that you come in for your meeting on time, that you complete all the sections on the form. That's the agreement we have, and you're asking me to break that.

Claimant #1   No, you're asking me to apply for jobs which would mean leaving my five-year-old son at home alone with nobody to look after him. With no food, no gas or electricity and the landlord on the phone about his rent – which he has now increased for the second time this year and for which you're giving me no help. If you want me to meet the agreement, then don't criminalize me for being a

Claimant #3   Because my mobility allowance has been cut and it was all the way over in Wembley.

Client Advisor #3   Well, we don't deal with mobility allowance, this is the Jobcentre.

Claimant #3   I know that, but both my mobility allowance and my DLA have been cut, and that's why I couldn't . . . –

Client Advisor #3   There isn't DLA now, there's only PIP.

Claimant #3   Yes I know, that's what my health check was for.

fucking parent when I'm doing everything I can to find something, anything at all, and which you refuse to take into account as if raising a child is some sort of luxury. It's not my fault there's nothing out there that fits round his school hours. My son finishes school at 3.15, there's nothing I can do about that. And when I can't afford to put him in after-school clubs then I don't see why I should have to be penalized every time I come in . . . –

Client Advisor #1   Alright, just one second.

Claimant #1   Excuse me, sorry . . . ?

Client Advisor #2 is sitting with **Claimant #2** *at a desk.* **Client Advisor #2** *is reading through* **Claimant #2***'s claim forms.*

Client Advisor #3   Right, and at the same time that the PIP health check came back and told us that you're not eligible for its mobility component, the ESA health check also determined that you're fit and ready to work.

Claimant #3   I've been looking for work since I left school.

Client Advisor #3   Well you're not going to get anything if you don't turn up for your interviews.

Claimant #3   I just told you, that's why I need mobility allowance.

Client Advisor #1 Give me a moment, give me a second?

Client Advisor #1 gets up and exits, leaving Claimant #1 stranded at the desk.

Client Advisor #3 re-enters and sits at the desk, holding Claimant #1's booklet and another form.

The dialogue continues . . .

Claimant #1 I'm sorry, who are you?

Client Advisor #3 Let's just be clear, Debbie, yeah? The time I've got down on your agreement here . . . .

Claimant #2 You know I've been sitting here for the best part of twenty minutes.

Client Advisor #2 Have you got somewhere else to be?

Claimant #2 Well, I'd rather be out out looking for a job. Do you have any?

Client Advisor #2 What?

Claimant #2 Here at the Jobcentre. Maybe I could do what you do? No offence, but it doesn't look too taxing.

Client Advisor #2 You wouldn't want to work here. Would you give me a moment.

Client Advisor #3 I'm sorry, could you continue this with my colleague?

Claimant #3 What?

Client Advisor #3 If you could wait one moment please?

Client Advisor #3 *gets up and exits, leaving* **Claimant #3** *stranded at the desk.*

Claimant #1   It says 2.30, I've just been through all this with your colleague.

Client Advisor #3   Yes, and if you're going to be aggressive we have the right to pass you to a third party.

Claimant #1   Who's being aggressive, sorry?

Client Advisor #3   2.30 *was* the agreed time.

Claimant #1   No, not agreed actually, I've already explained to your colleague, as well as calling you on the phone this morning. My son finishes school at 3.15 so to call me in

Claimant #2   What?

Client Advisor #2   One moment please.

Client Advisor #2 *gets up and exits, leaving* **Claimant #2** *stranded at the desk.*

for a 2.30 meeting is completely out of the question . . . –

Client Advisor #3 Well there's no record of it.

Claimant #1 What?

Client Advisor #3 There's no record that you called. You didn't call through to this desk.

Claimant #1 No, because they said they'd pass the message on to the relevant whoever. Ask your colleague.

Client Advisor #3 Look, there's just nothing on our system and so we have to put it down, we . . . have to treat it as

Client Advisor #1 *enters and sits at the desk.*

Claimant #2 Sorry, are you ready to deal with me now?

Client Advisor #1 That's what we're doing, we're dealing with your case.

Claimant #2 'My case', that's got a nice ring to it. Sounds like a court order.

Client Advisor #1 Well, we do have to abide by the law. We do have to look into why you're still claiming.

Client Advisor #2 *enters and sits at the desk.*

Client Advisor #2 Okay, so you've been refused mobility allowance on account of your health assessment?

Claimant #3 I wouldn't call it an assessment. The woman, the medical professional whoever she was, she asked me to sit on a table and raise my hand

a failure to attend your meeting.

Claimant #1   And I had to pick up my son.

Client Advisor #3   And that sets everybody back – me, my colleagues, the other claimants. Imagine if you were ten minutes late for a job interview . . . –

Claimant #1   So what should I do exactly? Put him up for adoption? The least I can do is be there to pick him up at the end of the day.

Client Advisor #3   Isn't there anybody else who could do it? Family, friends?

Claimant #2   You know my last job interview was nine months ago?

Client Advisor #2   Yes, and that's why we need more evidence to determine if you're fulfilling your role as a jobseeker.

Claimant #2   Listen, I've got ten GCSE's, an English degree and I've also completed an MA at Birkbeck University. So not only am I qualified, I've also got debts this bloody big to cheer me on. I apply for ten jobs a week, twenty jobs a fortnight. That's four hundred jobs each year for roughly how long now?

above my head. She didn't ask me anything about my mobility problems.

Client Advisor #2   Your learning difficulties.

Claimant #3   No, my mobility problems.

Client Advisor #2   Well, the health-check does consider everything I think.

Claimant #2   Look, you've got the letter from my doctor about all this . . . –

Client Advisor #2   I know it's frustrating, but I can only do my job.

Claimant #1 I've used up all my favours unfortunately. How about you go and pick him up?

Client Advisor #3 Look, I'm just doing my bit, giving you the instructions. If you don't want to attend, that's fine.

Claimant #1 I do want to attend, that's the point.

Client Advisor #3 Okay, but just so you know, if you do fail to turn up for our meeting again then I will shut down your claim within five working days.

Claimant #1 Why, because you're afraid you won't meet your targets? Tell me, how

Client Advisor #1 Twenty-eight months.

Claimant #2 Right, so you can sit there for as long as you want. Check, double-check my case all day long, but I'm telling you now there is nothing, literally nothing out there. And I've got debts. You seem intelligent enough, surely I shouldn't have to point that out to you?

Client Advisor #1 Well, I do know how tough it is, I have to work two jobs myself.

Claimant #2 Well do let me know if you ever need cover won't you?

Claimant #3 What's frustrating is that I can't rely on my mum to take time off from work to drive me around every day. That's why I needed my mobility allowance.

Client Advisor #2 Mobility component. You need to take that up with the PIP, look on the yougov website. In the meantime, I'm here to try and help you get back to work.

Claimant #3 Back to work? How can I work if I can't get to work?

Client Advisor #1 McDonald's in Finsbury Park are looking for someone.

many sanctions have they asked you to hand out today? Five maybe? Ten?

Client Advisor #3   You lean over my desk one more time and I will call security.

Claimant #3   I told you I can't do that.

Client Advisor #1   You've got a problem with McDonald's?

Claimant #3   I've got a problem getting to Finsbury Park.

Client Advisor #2   Well if that's the case then I'm afraid we won't be able to give you the ESA allowance either. Perhaps if we were to give you a couple of months while you sorted out your travel arrangements? Then maybe we can start this conversation again?

Claimant #3   And how am I supposed to live in the meantime?

Liam *exits*.

20.

The park.

Afternoon.

In the distance, the sound of a class of primary school children singing R. Kelly's 'The Greatest' from their classroom, accompanied by the school piano. **Liam** *quickly enters, rucksack over his shoulder.*

He moves to the bushes and dumps the rucksack on the ground.

He removes his blazer, shirt and tie, dumping them on the ground and kicking them into the bushes.

Liam *opens the rucksack and removes his t-shirt and hoodie and proceeds to put them on, as . . .*

The **Teenage Boy** (*from Scene 8*) *enters from the same direction that* **Liam** *first entered.*

He wears a cap/hat, and still has his bag. Again, he has half a spliff in his hand, which he occasionally puffs from, and he is texting on his phone.

The **Teenage Boy** *moves to a log/stump and sits, texting and smoking the spliff.*

Pause.

Liam, *on seeing the* **Teenage Boy**, *stops what he's doing and hesitates, not sure which way to turn.*

Pause.

Teenage Boy *takes a pull from the spliff, then offers it to* **Liam**.

Pause.

Liam   Nah, yeah.

Liam *finishes putting on his hoodie.*

He picks up his rucksack and moves over to the **Teenage Boy**.

He takes the spliff, takes a pull.

Long pause, as the **Teenage Boy** *continues texting.*

Liam*, who hasn't really smoked any of the spliff, offers it back to* **Teenage Boy***, but he doesn't notice.*

Liam *continues to loiter by the* **Teenage Boy***, holding the spliff and occasionally taking a pull.*

Long pause.

Teenage Boy (*texting, not looking up from phone*)   You remember Tia init?

Liam   Oh, . . . –

Teenage Boy   Tia, in our year. Green eyes.

Liam   Nah, fuck nah, Tia. Green eyes.

Teenage Boy   So she got fucked by ten guys last night?

Beat.

Teenage Boy   At least ten.

Liam   Oh yeah, isit?

Liam *offers the spliff back again. This time, the* **Teenage Boy** *takes it.*

Still texting, he pulls on the joint.

21.

Sainsbury's.

Dusk.

Bright lights inside, getting dark outside.

By the self-checkout machines.

A half-dozen or so shoppers are using the self-checkout machines, or queuing for the machines. A Sainsbury's security guard stands close by, checking his mobile phone most of the time. A Sainsbury's shopping assistant stands close to the checkout machines, tidying up baskets and occasionally helping shoppers by moving over to a checkout machine and tapping in an authorization code on one of the screens. Sainsbury's shopping music.

Apart from **Teenage Boy** *and* **Liam***'s dialogue, the only other noise is from the Sainsbury's shopping music from the store speakers, as well as the robotic voices from the self-checkout machines instructing the shoppers where to put their bags, when to collect their change, etc. The robotic voices are accompanied by various blips, whirrs and beeps from the machines.*

There may also be sounds from customer activity from the rest of the shopping centre too.

Liam *and the* **Teenage Boy***, both with bags over their shoulders, are queuing up for a free self-checkout machine. They're holding crisps, a chocolate milk drink, bars of chocolate, and a* Walking Dead *DVD.*

Both are stoned, particularly **Liam***.*

Liam *holds a bottle of orange juice which he has already opened and drinks from, whilst listening to the* **Teenage Boy** *who, from the start of the scene, talks incessantly, whilst constantly checking and rechecking his phone for messages . . .*

Teenage Boy   – . . . system, brov, the system's going to fuck you. Come out of school and they expect you to work for free? You think I'm going to bust my arse on some training course when there aint . . . –

The **Teenage Boy***'s phone bleep-bleeps – a text message. The* **Teenage Boy** *checks the message as he talks . . .*

Teenage Boy   – When there aint nothing at the end of it, the fuck is that? Yeah, go work voluntary five days a week so that they might not sanction you. Nah, man, got to play by your own rules init? Aint no one in the real world who's not out to fuck you. Everywhere you look, from every side.

Liam   Like every side init?

Teenage Boy   And they're like 'We're going to buy you out, bruv. We're going to buy up all the nice old houses, the schools, the jobs.' Bistros and shit, health centres, cycle shops, estate agents. Look around you, G. Moving in, driving up the prices. They're the real migrants, cuz, not them brothers hiding under trucks in Calais. It's these 50k bitches with their recycled bags, driving up and down in their Range Rovers, they're the problem, G. And you know someday there aint going to be no one left? Can't afford to live here no more, so they push us all out to some fucked-up EDL ghetto down in Thornton Heath so that they can go on with their lives without having to look reality in the face and I'm like 'What? Fuck off man, the fuck you are. I aint going nowhere, G.' Gotta find your own means, brov. Go work for the other side, you know what I'm saying? Mandem making plenty dollars and they aint going to threaten you with sanctions. Aint going to drive you out your home or make you work like a bitch until you're sixty fucking five years old. Look at my dad. Working the night shift over in Gatwick his whole life, never doing shit with shit, and I'm thinking to myself 'fuck man . . . –'

Liam   Fuck man.

Teenage Boy   Like for what? Shit, man, like I respect you and everything? I respect how much you put in, how hard you work at your job . . . –

Liam   Yeah, respect.

Teenage Boy   If you've nothing to show for it? Like you followed all the dots and that's it?

No reward, no nothing. Swallowed up by the system, brov.

Liam   Nah, fuck . . . –

Teenage Boy   'Cause that's how they plan it, cuz, the network. Look at Syria n'shit, Isis. All them man are in on the deal, there aint no war. It's all about keeping the top tier up. Pyramids, fam, networks. There aint no way I'm going to be pushed out.

The **Teenage Boy** *types a quick reply to the text message in his phone, as . . . –*

Teenage Boy   Want to be up there. Up in the four per cent, cuz, the elite. Want to get my own pool someday. Roof gardens. Tennis courts.

Liam   Computer.

Teenage Boy   What?

Liam   Yeah, just . . . – What you said init.

Teenage Boy   Man, your eyes are red-up.

Liam   Eh? Yeah, I don't know . . . –

Teenage Boy (*laughs*)   Fuck man, you like some devil, look.

Teenage Boy *points his phone at* **Liam**, *takes a picture.*

Liam   Oh nah man, don't . . . –

Teenage Boy   Like Darth Maul or some shit. – Nah nah, wait . . . –

The **Teenage Boy** *shows* **Liam** *his picture on the screen.*

Teenage Boy (*laughs*)   True-dat init!

Liam (*laughs*)   Ah, shit, really?

Teenage Boy   True-dat! Fam, you are baked, G, that is too funny.

The **Teenage Boy**'s *mobile phone bleep-bleeps – a text message.*

Liam (*still laughing*)   What, so like Darth Maul then a bit, like a beast?

The **Teenage Boy** *reads his text,* **Liam** *is still laughing/giggling.*

Liam (*still laughing*)   Like some devil or something then, . . . –

Teenage Boy   Yeah, like two minutes?

The **Teenage Boy** *hands rucksack, his chocolate/crisps and the* Walking Dead *DVD to* **Liam,** *who is still giggling, then zips up his top.*

Teenage Boy   Wait here two minutes.

Liam (*still giggling*)   Oh . . . –

Teenage Boy   I'll be back in ten minutes. Here . . . –

The **Teenage Boy** *pulls a handful of cash from his pocket and gives it to* **Liam.**

Teenage Boy   Pay for my t'ings though init? Yo, get your shit together, G, I'll see you by the bus stop.

Liam (*trying to control giggling*)   Okay, then cool . . . –

Teenage Boy   And don't be like drinking up my chocolate milk there. Ten minutes.

Liam (*trying to control giggling*)   Nah nah, ten minutes then, fam.

The **Teenage Boy** *quickly exits* (*out of the shop*).

Liam, *still trying to control his giggling, struggles to hold onto the* **Teenage Boy***'s bag, the food and the money.*

He's stoned, self-conscious, and at the front of the queue – the music and the noise from the self-checkout machines continues.

Long pause.

A light flashes green at the top of one of the self-checkout machines, indicating that it's free.

Liam *hesitates, then moves forward to the machine.*

He stares at the machine.

Hesitates, then starts scanning the items.

He scans the crisps, then the chocolate milk drink, and – beep . . .

Self-checkout machine   Please place item in bagging area.

*He hesitates, then places the crisps down on the scanning area, and
– beep . . .*

Self-checkout machine   Please place item in bagging area.

Liam *puts the chocolate milk drink in the bagging area.*

Self-checkout machine   Unexpected item in bagging area.

Liam *hesitates, then puts the crisps in the bagging area.*

Self-checkout machine   Unexpected item in bagging area.

Liam *takes everything out of the bagging area, and – beep . . .*

Self-checkout machine   Assistance needed.

Pause.

Liam *tries scanning the DVD – beep, and . . .*

Self-checkout machine   Assistance needed.

He hesitates.

Liam *places the item in the bagging area, and . . .*

Self-checkout machine   Unexpected item in bagging area.

Liam *picks up the item, as . . .*

Self-checkout machine   Please place item in bagging area.

He tries to scan the DVD, as . . .

Self-checkout machine   Assistance required.

He puts the DVD in the bagging area, as . . .

Self-checkout machine   Unexpected item in bagging area.

Liam *picks up the DVD, as the* **Shopping Assistant** *moves over
to him.*

The **Shopping Assistant** *takes the DVD from* **Liam***.*

Efficiently, the **Shopping Assistant** *removes the protective case
(with a key from his/her keyring) and scans the DVD.*

Liam   Nah, cool, that's . . . –

Self-checkout machine   Please select payment type. Have you swiped your Nectar card?

The **Shopping Assistant** *returns to his/her spot.*

Pause.

Liam *hesitates, then . . . –*

Self-checkout machine   Please select payment type. Have you swiped your Nectar card?

He takes the money that the **Teenage Boy** *gave him. There is a twenty-pound note.*

Self-checkout Machine   Please select payment . . . –

He feeds the notes into the machine.

Pause.

The machine spits out his note.

Liam *takes it, smooths it out.*

He inserts the note.

Pause.

Self-checkout machine   Have you swiped your Nectar card? Please take your change.

Notes are dispensed under the scanner.

The machine spits out a receipt and change.

Liam *struggles to take his change, placing his bag in the bagging area as he does so.*

Self-checkout machine   Unexpected item in bagging area.

Liam *removes his bag, putting it over his shoulder, along with the* **Teenage Boy***'s rucksack.*

Clumsily, **Liam** *picks up the DVD and the snacks, holding them in both hands and wedging them under his arms.*

He exits, moving past the shoppers and the self-checkout machines, stuffing the snacks into his pockets.

22.

Bus stop on Church Road.

Dusk.

Flashing blue lights from nearby police car.

Sound of police walkie-talkies, sirens and other traffic close by.

Smashed glass on the floor from the shelter. Other debris.

The Teenage Boy's trainer or jacket on the ground.

The bus shelter is cordoned off with police tape. A crime scene.

A **Policeman** *stands at the corner of the crime scene, keeping pedestrians away from the crime scene, his walkie-talkie in hand.*

An old woman stands at a distance, with her shopping holdall.

Liam *enters with both rucksacks and the snacks, some/most of them stuffed in his pockets.*

He is blocked by the police tape and sees the crime scene.

Policeman   You want to cross at the crossing.

Pause.

Policeman   Go back and cross at the crossing, there's access the other side.

Liam   Access the other side.

The two **Schoolgirls** *enter, and exit as quickly as they come on.*

Pause.

Liam (*to the* **Policeman**) Nah, yeah.	**Schoolgirl #2** (*as they enter*) Ah fuck man, look at this.
Pause.	**Schoolgirl #1** (*as they exit*) I told you we should've waited for the 3.
Liam (*to the* **Policeman**) Cool then cool.	
Liam *hesitates, then turns and exits the way he came.*	**Schoolgirl #2** (*as they exit*) When did you say that? You never opened your mouth once.

23.

A wall, by a busy road, near a school.

Early evening.

Sounds of traffic close by, etc.

Mysha, *9 years old, is sitting on the wall, in her school uniform.*

She is playing Angry Birds on her phone. She has a packet of crisps and the chocolate milk on the wall next to her.

Liam *enters, both bags over his shoulder, and returns to his place back on the wall.*

Liam (*as he enters*)   Throw away your own wrappers next time.

He sits on the wall next to **Mysha**.

Liam   Bin is heaving, look.

He pulls out one of the chocolate bars from his pocket and unwraps it.

Mysha *continues playing Angry Birds, occasionally taking sips from the chocolate milk.*

Long pause.

Liam   Better eat them Doritos before I do init?

Pause.

Liam   Mysha.

Pause.

Liam   Mysha . . . –

Mysha   Yeah, I heard you man.

Liam   Supposed to be a treat.

Pause.

Liam *hesitates, then takes a couple of bites of the chocolate bar.*

Pause.

Liam   Like a treat though. Like an occasion sort of thing?

Pause.

Liam   Mysha.

Long pause.

Liam   Mysha . . .

Mysha   Yeah, I told you, I'm saving them for breakfast.

Liam   Aren't you hungry now?

Mysha   I got this milkshake for now. Let me just mash-up this green pig though.

Liam   Who?

Mysha   Let me just mash-up this green pig.

Mysha *tap-taps on the phone,* **Liam** *watches.*

Mysha   Arrr man, shit . . . –

Liam *takes the phone off* **Mysha***.*

Mysha   No, wait, I aint done.

Liam *tap-taps on the phone,* **Mysha** *tries to grab it back.*

He doesn't let her.

Mysha   Fuck man, I said I aint finished yet.

Liam *tap-taps.*

Mysha   I said I aint done, Liam man, give me my phone.

Mysha *goes to grab the phone,* **Liam** *holds it up, out of her reach, with . . .*

Liam   – Stay away from them boys.

Mysha   Who?

Liam   Nah, just . . . – Stay away from them boys, go the playground.

Mysha   Playground – What am I, four? Which boys?

Liam   You're eight.

Mysha   I'm nine, Liam, nine, it was my birthday in January. The fuck are you talking about?

Mysha *grabs the phone and continues tap-tapping on the screen.*

Mysha   Arr shit, man, you've messed the whole thing up now. Like the oldest app in the world and you have to fuck it up. Sounding like a muslim or something, 'Stay away from them boys' – you going mosque?

Liam   Nah.

Mysha   So stay out my business then, Liam, I swear. You know you're going to get blazed?

Liam   Nah, shut up.

Mysha   Shut up, man, it's true. You know I'm supposed to make my own way home now, Mum said. She's on zero hours now, her and my dad. One day I'm going to be on zero hours too, why do you think they went out and got me this phone? I can call home, childline, 999. You know this thing's got Skype, the fuck do I need you for?

Liam   I'm your older brother.

Mysha   You're not my brother.

Liam   Half-brother then.

Mysha   Yeah, and I can make my own way home.

Long pause.

Mysha   Need my own room n'shit.

Liam   Oh, right then do you?

Mysha   Need my own space now init? Want to invite my friends over sometime.

Liam   Why?

Mysha   All your shit everywhere still. You know you should get yourself a flat or something. Shit, man, your phone don't even work.

Liam   They aint your friends.

Mysha   What?

Liam   They're not your real friends are they?

Long pause.

Mysha   You look like you're going to cry.

Liam   Shut up, nah.

Mysha   You know you should get them Frijj shakes next time.

Mysha *gets up, grabs her bag.*

Mysha   Come then.

Pause.

Mysha   Come, I'm tired. Stuck in there all day. Breakfast club, after-school club.

Liam   Nah, cool then, I'm busy.

Mysha   Busy?

Liam   Make your own way then.

Mysha   Nah, fuck off, you aint busy.

Liam   I'm busy, alright?

Mysha   Busy since when? You are so full of shit.

Liam *gets up and quickly exits.*

Mysha   Yo, Liam man! Busy since when?

24.

Roadworks.

Evening.

Liam *enters.*

He is blocked by the roadworks – including traffic cones, signs.

Liam *exits the way he came.*

Pause.

Liam *re-enters.*

He barges through the roadworks, kicking over traffic cones, signs, as he goes.

Pause.

Liam *exits the way he came.*

25.

The bus stop on Church Road.

Early evening.

It is still cordoned off, but the police and flashing blue lights have gone.

Liam *enters.*

He looks around to see if anyone is nearby.

Pause.

He takes the Teenage Boy's bag off his shoulder, and places it by the bus stop.

Long pause.

He removes the change from his pocket, and goes to put it down on the ground.

Flashing blue lights and the sound of a passing police car.

Liam *pockets the change and exits.*

26.

A bus stop.

Evening.

A **Mother** *and a* **Sleepy Toddler**, *on the bench, waiting for a bus.*

The **Sleepy Toddler** *sits on the* **Mother**'s *knee. A pushchair close by.*

The **Mother** *holds a picture book and reads to the* **Sleepy Toddler**.

She speaks in a foreign, non-English, language (Polish, Farsi, Arabic, Urdu etc. depending on the actor's ethnicity).

Mother (*in a foreign language*)   . . . poor cat, thought Scrap. If only she could climb that tall tree, if only she wasn't so scared.

The **Mother** *turns a page, as* **Liam** *enters, sitting on the bench.*

Mother (*in a foreign language*)   And so Scrap thought, and thought, and he thought. And suddenly the wise old peacock's words came back to him again.

The **Mother** *turns a page, and* . . .

Mother (*in a foreign language*)   If at first you don't succeed, try try and try again.

The **Mother** *turns a page.*

Mother (*in a foreign language*)   'Oh, thank you, little doggy' said the Cat. 'Now I can sleep on my favourite branch all day long.' And so she did.

The **Mother** *turns a page.*

Mother (*in a foreign language*)   'But I still haven't found my bone!' cried Scrap. And he was just about to run back home, when . . . –

The **Mother** *turns a page.*

Mother (*in a foreign language*)   Oh dear!

The **Mother** *laughs, as* . . .

*A **Male Jogger** enters, in tracksuit bottos and a 'Better Gym' t-shirt, jogging.*

He stops by the bus stop . . .

Mother (*in a foreign language*)   Poor little monkey, thought Scrap. If only he could peel that banana, if only he wasn't so tired.

*The **Mother** turns a page, as **Liam** gets up and comes out of the shelter, watching **Doctor #1** as she disappears up the road.*

Male Jogger *takes a bottle of water from his hydration waist-pack, and glugs down a couple of mouthfuls.*

Liam *watches him.*

Male Jogger *sees **Liam** watching him.*

*He nods and taps **Liam** on the shoulder, as . . .*

Mother (*in a foreign language*) he thought, and he thought.

And so Scrap thought, and

Liam *gets up and exits, following **Male Jogger**.*

Mother (*in a foreign language*) peacock said?

Now what was it the wise old

27.

At the doctor's.

Day.

Doctor #2 *is sitting at his desk, typing on the computer. A **Young Student Doctor** is also sitting in the room, taking notes on a notepad.*

Liam *is also seated by the desk.*

Doctor #2   So you want to feel better. Do you mean physically or psychologically or both?

Long pause.

Doctor #2   If it's psychological, emotional . . . –

Liam   Good to feel better I think, yeah. Good to stay that way I think. Better all fucking round.

Doctor #2   And you want us to help with that?

Liam   Yeah, 'course. 'Course, nah, fuck.

Long pause.

Liam   Fuck.

Doctor #2   No, that's fine.

Liam   Fuck, sorry, just . . . –

Doctor #2   How healthy are you right now? Generally, I mean.

Liam   Generally yeah, the skills. (*To* **Student Doctor**.) Getting all them skills sort of thing, Rachel, init? (*To* **Doctor #2**.) Yeah, student doctor sort of thing, cool. Student doctor Rachel.

Long pause.

Doctor #2   Okay.

Pause.

Doctor #2   Okay, perhaps I should . . . –

Doctor #2 *types on the computer.*

Pause.

Doctor #2   I'm sorry, if you could just answer a few . . . –

Liam   A few then, cool.

Doctor #2   A few general questions for me, helps me to . . . – (*Back to* **Liam**.) Helps me to get a rough idea, is that alright? Anything we need to know.

Liam   Nah, wicked, that's wicked. General questions.

Doctor #2   Determine what kind of thing we might be able to offer you.

Liam   Determine away then, wicked.

Doctor #2   Okay, well on a scale of one to ten, and if if ten is excellent and five is average?

Beat.

Doctor #2   Don't worry, I'm just . . . –

Liam   Nah, eight.

Doctor #2   We're talking about your overall health. Physically, psychologically . . . –

Liam   Nah, eight, sir.

Doctor #2   Eight?

Liam   Yeah, seven eight, miss. Rachel, I mean.

Doctor #2 *types,* **Student Doctor** *jots down* **Liam***'s answers on the pad.*

Pause.

Liam   And so like ten's excellent then?

Doctor #2   They're just one or two preliminary questions.

Liam   Nah, awesome, I get that. Ten.

Doctor #2   And so you wouldn't say you'd been feeling down or listless? Lacking energy.

Liam   Energy? Nah not . . . –

Doctor #2 *holds up his hand, stopping* **Liam** *speaking, as he writes.*

Pause.

Liam   Just sort of, yeah. – (*To* **Student Doctor**.) Writing it all down then isn't he?

Doctor #2   You're not stressed or depressed about anything?

Liam   Nah, not . . . – Not anything I can think of, sir. – (*Mimics* **Doctor #2** *for* **Student Doctor**.) 'Stressed or depressed'.

Doctor #2   No suicidal thoughts?

Liam   Nah, fuck off, nothing.

Doctor #2   Nothing?

Liam   Nah just . . . – What you said. Nothing at all. – (*To* **Student Doctor**.) Positive sort of. Healthy.

Doctor #2   And if I were to ask you how you would describe your life in five years' time?

Liam   Okay, yeah? Yeah, okay . . . –

Doctor #2   If you could imagine that for me, Liam. Five years' time. Where you think you might be? The sort of things you might be doing, where you might be.

Liam   Right, cool.

Doctor #2   If you could just describe that for me.

Liam   Like in five years then?

Very long pause.

Doctor #2   That's okay, that's fine.

Pause.

Doctor #2   That's fine, Liam, take your time.

28.

The bus stop.

Morning.

There is some rain.

Two or three **Commuters**, *dressed for work, wait for the bus under the shelter.*

A couple of them tap and scroll on their iPhones, another sits staring at the road ahead.

Long pause.

Liam *enters, as before, with a pharmaceutical bag.*

He sits on the bench.

Long pause.

He opens the pharmaceutical bag, and takes out a box of tablets.

He opens and investigates the tablets, as . . .

Another couple of **Commuters** *enter, with perhaps umbrellas, bags and iPhones.*

They join the others under the shelter.

Long pause.

Another **Commuter** *enters, joins them under the shelter.*

Liam *can now hardly be seen.*

Long pause.

Another **Commuter** *enters . . .*

Followed by another **Commuter***.*

The **Commuters** *tap on their phones, stare at the road, shake an umbrella, read the paper, etc.*

Long pause.

Liam *cannot be seen.*

Lights fade.

The End.

Appendix

'Boy' is presented through Liam's perspective. Surrounding him are many characters, dialogues and actions.

There are 'simultaneous dialogues' in the main script and they should always be used in the play.

This appendix includes a selection of extra scenes (chronological and numbered as they are in the play) that you may also wish to use in the play. Most of them are written for the big 'train' and 'Victoria station' scenes, but feel free to use them in other moments of the play if that's useful.

Once more, the action plays simultaneously with the action in Liam's scenes, with the dialogue often overlapping, but never drowning out, the dialogue in the scene's central action.

Please feel free to use all or none or a little of the following extras.

2.

The doctor's waiting room.

Other actors can play **Patients** *who are sitting alone, quietly waiting, reading magazines, or on their phones, but below are several dialogues happening simultaneously – at varying paces/ speeds – as* **Liam** *passes through . . .*

A.

A second **Receptionist** *is answering a phone-call.*

Receptionist #3   Paxton Surgery. . . . Yes? . . . Okay, yeah, could I have your date of of birth please? . . . Right . . . Right, that's . . . Davenport is it?

. . . Okay . . . Okay, well I'll just have a look for you . . . I appreciate that, yes . . . – We're fairly busy at the moment I

know . . . Dr Chaudry's not in till tomorrow morning . . . If
you just – . . . Yep, I'm looking for them now, just . . . Okay,
hold the line for a moment please . . . Hold the line, Mr
Davenport, hold the line.

Receptionist #3 *presses a button and waits for an internal call to
be answered.*

Long pause.

Receptionist #3 *presses a button and returns to the original call.*

Receptionist #3   Hello, hi. . . . No, I'm afraid there's no
one answering the phone right now, do you want me to pass
on a message? . . . – Well, it'll be later today. . . . – Later
today, after lunchtime . . . If you call back at about two or
three. – . . . No, of course. – . . . Of course, yep, we'll do
that. . . . – Could you give me your name again please? . . . –
Right . . .

– No, I'll make sure he knows that . . . – No, we don't do that
I'm afraid. –

– Mm-hm . . . Mm, yes, well you can easily do that . . . You've
got the number for them as well have you?

B.

*An **Elderly Father** in his late seventies violently coughs, holding a
tissue to his mouth.*

*His **Grown-Up Daughter** sits next to him, magazine on her lap,
holding a bottle of water.*

Grown-Up Daughter   Why don't you drink some?

Pause.

Grown-Up Daughter   Drink some, come on.

Dad   I can't stand that bottled crap.

Grown-Up Daughter   It's just water.

Dad   Well, I don't know what's in it.

Grown-Up Daughter   Dad . . . –

Dad   Don't fuss for Christ'sakes, Ella.

Pause.

The **Elderly Father** *coughs again.*

Grown-Up Daughter   I bought it for you, Dad, please.

Dad   Don't wave it in front of my face.

Pause.

Elderly Father *rummages in his pocket and takes out a packet of throat lozenges.*

Dad   Got my sweets.

Elderly Father *puts a lozenge in his mouth and sucks.*

Dad   You want a sweet?

Grown-Up Daughter   No.

Dad   Take a sweet, go on.

Grown-Up Daughter   No thank you.

Pause.

Grown-Up Daughter   They're packed with sugar, Dad, I've told you before.

The **Father** *reads the label on the lozenges.*

Dad   Don't say nothing about sugar here.

C.

Two **Ladies** *in their late fifties/early sixties.* **Lady #1** *leans in to* **Lady #2** *talking constantly but quietly.* **Lady #1** *listens, nodding, sucking on a sweet, 'mm-ing' and 'oh-ing'.*

Lady #1   It isn't easy, no, she's always had problems. She's always had problems, that one, she takes after her dad's side of the family I think. Hopeless with money, hasn't managed to save a penny in over thirty years – even when she was working. I thought she was on her way to having a breakdown, but what do I know? Something's clicked.

Lady #2   Yeah.

Lady #1   Something's clicked along the way, I don't know how or why, but anyway.

Thing is, it's all fine now. Managed to keep that place on Church Road just about. Two bedrooms, nice size lounge. Not huge, but you know?

Enough, I think, for the purpose. Enough for what she needs . . . –

D.

A **Young Woman** *in loose clothing and a bobble hat enters quickly from one of the doctors' offices.*

She holds a prescription and a urine sample in a clear plastic bag.

She moves to the reception desk, and signals to **Receptionist #2**.

Young Woman   Sorry, do I put this . . . ?

Receptionist #2 *taps on a box.*

Young Woman   Oh .. – Thanks, thankyou.

Young Woman *places the urine sample in the box.*

She quickly exits the surgery.

5.

The park. A woody, secluded spot.

At the tail-end of the scene a **Woman in Tracksuit and Cap***, smoking a cigarette and holding a phone to her ear, enters.*

She hurriedly walks along the muddy path, past **Liam** *and* **Man With Dog***, talking on the phone to an automated call, until she exits.*

Woman in Tracksuit *and* **Cap** (*on phone*)   . . . Yes! . . . No! . . . Tax Credits! . . . Yes!

. . . Child Tax Credits! . . . No! . . . To speak to someone! . . .
Yes! . . . Yes!

6.

The bus stop.

A.

Two **Schoolboys**, *in uniform, with schoolbags, are close by the*
Shelter, waiting for the bus.

Schoolboy #1 *is kneeling on the floor, attempting to remove a*
fleece from his schoolbag without all his books falling out. Once
the fleece is out, he has to remove his blazer, put the fleece on, and
then put the blazer back on (on top of the fleece). He makes this
harder for himself by holding, and occasionally drinking from an
opened bottle of Lucozade.

His friend, **Schoolboy #2**, *also has a drink – a carton – wedged in*
his blazer pocket, and he holds a packet of crisps which he constantly
crunches on.

He also has a fleece, tied round his waist.

Schoolboy #2 *is laughing at* **Schoolboy #1**.

Schoolboy #2   You aint going to make it.

Schoolboy #2 *crunches crisps, entertained by* **Schoolboy #1**'s
efforts with the fleece.

Schoolboy #2   That aint happening man, whassup with
you? Oh my days.

Schoolboy #1   Shut up, I'm doing it.

Schoolboy #2   'They wanna mash it up, woah!'

Schoolboy #2 *kicks* **Schoolboy #1**'s *bag.*

Schoolboy #1   Oi!

Schoolboy #2   'They wanna mash it up, woah!'

Schoolboy #2 *kicks* **Schoolboy #1**'s *bag.*

Schoolboy #1   Fuck, don't be doing that to my bag man.
The fuck you doing that to my stuff for?

Schoolboy #1 *retrieves his bag, hitting* **Schoolboy #2** *on the leg
as he does so.*

Schoolboy #2 *is still laughing at his friend, with a mouthful of
crisps.*

Pause.

Schoolboy #1 (*to the bag, fleece, etc.*)   Arrr come on.

Schoolboy #2   You should do what I do and tie it round
your waist.

Pause.

Schoolboy #2   Tie it, hang it round your waist man, I'm
telling you that's sense.

Schoolboy #1 *is finally on his feet, pulling the blazer over his
fleece, as* **Schoolboy #2**, *still eating, moves to the shelter and starts
randomly kicking it, rapping Drake's 'Know Yourself' to himself as
he does so.*

Schoolboy #1, *having finished putting his blazer on and putting
his bag on his back, turns and grabs* **Schoolboy #2**'s *fleece from his
waist and tries yanking it off, laughing.*

Schoolboy #2   Arr, you're bad man! You're . . . –

The **Schoolboys** *play a kind of tug-o'-war with the fleece,
aggressively, but laughing.*

Schoolboy #2   – . . . bad now init?!

Schoolboy #1 *manages to swipe the fleece, and darts round the
back of the shelter with it.* **Schoolboy #2** *chases him, and, behind
the bus shelter, crashes into his friend and grabs the fleece. They keep
wrestling for it, laughing.*

Schoolboy #2 (*as they wrestle*)   Nah, fuck off man!

Schoolboy #1 Ow! Fucking hell . . . –

Schoolboy #2 Bad man, let go of it. Let go of it, what's wrong with you? Fucking hell man, come on, look . . .

Schoolboy #2 *grabs his fleece back, as the bus approaches.*

Schoolboy #2 Yeah, you coming to mine?

Schoolboy #1 What now?

Schoolboy #2 Jump on the 3 man, you said.

Schoolboy #1 When did I say? I never said.

Schoolboy #2 Watch the *Star Wars* trailer.

Schoolboy #1 Eh?

Schoolboy #2 Half an hour. Come and watch the new *Star Wars* trailer with me, your mum aint home till five at least, she won't care. Jusr watch where you're tramping your feet though init?

B.

A **Commuter** *arrives at the bus stop, who has his/her mobile pressed to his/her ear throughout the scene, but only speaks a couple of times . . .*

Second Commuter (*on phone throughout*)   . . . No, I'll wait, I'm happy to wait.

. . .

. . .

. . .

. . . Hi there, hi.

. . .

. . .

. . .

. . . Yeah, that's fine, I'd rather – . . . Yep, speak directly, yep.
. . . No, it was just the recorded message. Alright, great.
Great, yeah.

. . .

. . .

. . .

. . .

. . . Hello?

. . .

. . .

. . .

. . .

. . . Hello? Yep, no, I'm still here.

. . .

. . .

. . .

8.

The bus stop (same as before).

As **Liam** *eats the chicken remains, cyclists in cycling gear and pushing mountain bikes walk down the road, past* **Liam** *and the* **Teenage Boy***, talking as they go.*

Cyclist #3　. . . it's the festival in Lille, we go there every year.

Cyclist #2　Lille, wow. You know that's one place I've never . . .

Cyclist #1　All-night drinking, the whole town . . . –

Cyclist #2   Really? Lille, wow.

Cyclist #3   Great for picking up bits and pieces, Katie loves it. She gets the Eurostar with the kids . . . –

Cyclist #1   You only need one day, so you know?

Cyclist #3   We were there in September, it's a pretty awesome ride.

Cyclist #1   And the whole town shuts down, it's just this great atmosphere. Hardly any English.

Cyclist #3   It's mobbed, but it's just really . . . –

Cyclist #1   No police, no violence, just this really cool vibe. Like a cloud of marijuana smoke and no one cares . . .

Cyclist #2   Arr Christ, guys, you've got to let me know, I'd be so onto that.

Cyclist #3   Can you imagine that in this fucking country? They'd have the batons and the shields out.

Cyclist #1   And the roads are really quiet. You don't have everyone trying to cut you down. Calais's a bit nut-driving I guess.

9.

The balcony/walkway.

Towards the end of the scene, around the 'Could you step away from the door now, please?' *section between* **Paula** *and* **Liam***, the following dialogue between* **Blonde Woman** *and* **Topless Man** *can be heard from within the* **Blonde Woman***'s flat.*

The dialogue should be offstage, muffled.

Topless Man   – . . . that's just the way they stay though init? I can't tell you how many hours I've wasted in there.

Blonde Woman   Yeah, that's how they stay, Jermaine,
you're right. Would you mind turning that shit off for a bit?
It's porno. I've told you before, I don't want my kid . . . –

Topless Man   Nah, man, you call this porn?

Blonde Woman   Yeah, and I've told you before I don't like
her being exposed to that stuff, it's degrading.

Topless Man   Oh, listen to you with your big words.

Blonde Woman   Look, just fuck off alright? – Turn it
off . . . –

Topless Man   'Ey, alright! No need to . . . –

Blonde Woman   Turn it off, you don't live here.

Topless Man   No need to fucking pull my hand off as soon
as you walk through the door. You know if you don't like
it . . . –

Blonde Woman   Nah, I don't like it.

Topless Man   Fine, so the bitch don't like it then, fuck it.

Blonde Woman   Where you going now?

Topless Man   The fuck do you care? Pretend like I don't
exist if you want to have your little blow-out in front of
the kid.

Blonde Woman   Yeah nice, Jermaine, you see this? Fuck
off, yeah? You see this? Fuck off, geddit?

Topless Man   You know I swear sometimes you're a bloke.

Blonde Woman   Yeah, so you're going to walk out the door
again? Jermaine.

Pause.

Blonde Woman   Jermaine . . . –

Topless Man   I'm getting you the key for fucksake,
'walking out'.

11B.

On the train.

Possible other dialogues littered around the carriage.

A.

The **Man in a Suit** *(in his late forties), talking to a* **Woman in a Suit** *(in her late thirties). Looking out of the window, in mid-conversation . . .*

Woman in a Suit   I wouldn't say no.

Man in a Suit   Of course you wouldn't say no. I don't think there's anyone in his right mind who'd say no.

Woman in a Suit   Her mind.

Man in a Suit   Sorry?

Woman in a Suit   You don't think anyone in his or her mind.

Man in a Suit   Oh, yes, the equality police, my mistake.

Woman in a Suit   Thank you.

Man in a Suit   Nothing like a bit of empty feminism to end the day.

Woman in a Suit   Hardly.

Man in a Suit   I actually think you'll find I'm quite the Suffragette in my old age.

Woman in a Suit   Terrible film. You know I could see you being quite happy up there.

Thirty storeys up.

Man in a Suit   Away from other humans, you mean. Windows all around, stood there looking down on the scum. Naked, of course.

Woman in a Suit   Premium real estate.

Man in a Suit   Well, yeah, they'll do for about one and a half million quid. Twenty-odd floors sitting empty. Two-bedroom flats, three-bedroom flats, penthouses up the top. Qatari-owned, just like everything else now.

Woman in a Suit   Yeah, they own the Shard.

Man in a Suit   The Shard, yeah, that's Qatari.

Liam   Qatari, yeah.

Man in a Suit   Some little Arab Prince on his jollies while I'm making myself sick for that little fucking studio in Wandsworth.

More people/commuters get on the carriage, finding seats or standing around them.

Woman in a Suit   You're sure you wouldn't rather I came back with you?

Man in a Suit   Deadline, sorry. Going to be online all night going from one atrocity to the other. Beheadings, murder, that sort of thing. You know that some of them use razor wire to take off the heads. I don't even care any more.

B.

At the same time, simultaneously, a beautiful couple in their late twenties, both scrolling and tapping on their iPads.

Young Woman   Share to buy makes more sense.

Young Man   I don't know, I haven't come across anything.

Young Man   There's got to be a website somewhere. It can't just be find-a-property-dot-com.

Young Woman   That's the main one I think.

Young Man   Thornton Heath, South Croydon.

Young Woman   I'm not living in Thornton Heath, that's totally out of our way. Who do we know lives in Croydon?

Young Man   They're the only places even remotely affordable.

Young Woman   Oh my god, we're fucked.

Young Man   And we'd still be looking at thirty grand for a deposit.

Young Woman   Where the hell are we going to get thirty grand? We've barely got fifty quid after all the direct debits every month.

Young Man   I don't know, I'll keep looking.

Young Woman   We should have saved.

Young Man   Yep.

Young Woman   We should have saved while we had the chance.

Young Man   And our parents should have saved for us.

Young Woman   I want to go north of the river, I hate the south. Isn't there anywhere in Muswell Hill or East Finchley?

Young Man   You're looking at five hundred thousand pounds, and that's for a one-bedroom.

Young Woman   Finsbury Park? Walthamstow?

Young Man   You're still looking at three hundred thousand in Hackney.

Young Woman   Then how did Sarah get her place?

Young Man   Because she bought in the 1990s. Peabody. Housing Association.

Young Woman   We need to do that. We should apply to our Housing Association.

Young Man   There's about a five-year waiting list. Unless it's extreme circumstances.

Young Woman   And you're telling me these aren't extreme circumstances?

Young Man   Nope.

Young Woman   What?

Young Man   We've got an income, we're married.

Young Woman   And we're going to be renting for the rest of our lives. Thirteen hundred pounds every month.

Young Man   We could always stay with my parents for a while. Try and save a bit of . . . –

Young Woman   Don't even go there.

Long pause.

The **Man** *shows the* **Woman** *something on his iPad screen.*

Woman   Wow. That's ridiculous.

Man   I would love that. Fix it up across the main wall.

Woman   It's massive.

Man   I know it's massive. THX sound.

Woman   Well, I wouldn't love that.

Man   Oh, get lost, you would. Season five of *The Walking Dead* on blu-ray.

Woman   I hate *The Walking Dead*.

Man   You don't hate *The Walking Dead*. It'd be our own little Multiplex.

Woman   Except we'd never actually leave.

Pause.

Woman   And you'd love that.

Man   I would, yeah.

They continue scrolling/tapping on their iPads, as the **Young Muslim Man** *enters the scene.*

Pause.

Woman   What do you think of this lamp?

Man   Nice, yeah. Retro.

C.

Two **Male Friends** *and a* **Female Friend**.

Male Friend #1   – . . . really nice because we're finally getting somewhere with it now, it's not just some excuse to doss about or whatever.

Male Friend #2   Not that it's ever been an excuse.

Female Friend   Oh god no . . .

Male Friend #1   Yeah, right, I mean if either one of us ever needed an excuse.

Male Friend #2   We wouldn't need to come up with a whole bloody team of people.

We wouldn't have invested all that money . . . –

Male Friend #1   Literally everything, he's put everything into this, Maria, it's just amazing.

Male Friend #2   Yeah, and because I knew it's a bloody good idea, that's why. – I mean, Christ knows where she gets off because I know she doesn't even believe what she's saying any more, it's just . . . –

Male Friend #1   Bitterness, resentment.

Male Friend #2   She doesn't get it, it's like . . . –

Female Friend   No, I mean, that's ridiculous, yeah.

Male Friend #2   Totally off the radar as far as she's concerned.

Male Friend #1   It's New Media.

Male Friend #2   New Media and she doesn't get it, she's coming up to seventy years old now.

Male Friend #1   His dad gets it, he's cool.

Female Friend   Oh really?

Male Friend #2   No, he's cool.

Male Friend #2   Well he says he does at least – I mean, come on, we've done that, we were dossing about for years.

Female Friend   Like anyone.

Male Friend #2   Like anyone, yeah. Like anyone that age.

Female Friend   Obligatory for fucksake.

Male Friend #1   And now we're that bit older, and we've got this like amazing thing at our disposal . . . –

More people/commuters get on the carriage, finding seats or standing around them.

Male Friend #2   It's fine, it's understandable. They're from a completely different . . . –

Female Friend   Mindset, yeah.

Male Friend #1   It's an amazing amazing thing that's happening right now. You've got Soundcloud, Haystack, Flotones, Mog . . . –

Male Friend #2   Jamnow, Sonific.

Male Friend #1   Sonific, yeah.

Female Friend   Wow.

Male Friend #1   And if you pull all these sites together, if you find a way of sharing all that information and bringing it all together . . .

D.

A couple in their thirties passing through the carriage.

Him   – . . . only two stops, better than changing platforms. You alright?

Her   Yeah, fine.

Him   Sorry I've made such a pig's ear of things tonight.

Her   Oh Christ, no, it's not your fault.

Him   I'm actually hoping this might be quicker in the end. Here, do you want to . . . ?

Her   No no, I've got everything I think. Have you got the thing with the address on?

Him   It's saved on my phone. Good old google maps.

Her   Cool, no, okay. I think there's seats through here?

E.

An **Older Man** *talking on his mobile, who also stands near the doorway.*

Older Man (*on phone*)   . . . Nah, nothing . . . Busy, yeah . . . I don't know, you? . . .

Okay, well that makes two of us then . . . No, not really . . .

Can't really talk . . . I said I can't really . . . – Yeah . . . No, it is.

. . . – I don't know, an hour? . . . – Yeah, you go ahead yeah. . . . – Yeah, probably . . . Mm-mm, yep . . . – See how it goes – . . . See what we think, yeah . . . – Pretty full-on, pretty tired . . . – Seems to be going around I think, yeah . . . – Okay . . . Okay then, yeah.

F

An **Older Woman** *enters carrying a large bag with a giant toy in it, looking for a seat.*

Older Woman   Sorry, can I squeeze . . . ? – Can I just get in . . . ? – Can I get in there? Thank you, thanks.

12.

The barriers by the main concourse.

There are lots of commuters, passing through the barriers – touching in (or out) with their Oyster cards.

Most are silent, possibly an occasional 'thanks', 'thank you', but you might include . . . –

A.

Person on Phone   . . . Yep, on my way. Yeah, just got off the train now, stay where you are, okay? . . . Yeah, great . . . Great, yeah, just wait there . . . On the concourse, just where you are, I'm . . . –

B.

Another Person to Another   . . . and then there's all the others who are just going to drag us right back down . . . –

Another Person to Another #2   Back to this time last year.

Another Person to Another   I swear to god, it's such a fucking waste . . . –

C.

Female Friend   . . . nah just, taking some time out I think, it's been such a god-awful year for me personally. Not that I'm particularly pissed off about anything in particular I don't think.

D.

Older Woman   No no, you're fine, go ahead . . . –

E.

Someone on Phone   . . . like trying to play Soduko with the Red Arrows or something, mad . . . Nah, mate, I know . . . – Nah, I know you are. – I know that about you, yeah.

F.

Him   Good timing actually. Are you alright?

Her   Yeah fine, fine, I've got it, don't worry.

Him   Good bloody timing.

G.

Friend to Friend   Need to go and use the cashpoint first.

Friend to Friend #2   Sure, yeah, go for it. Yeah, I think I'll just run to the Costa if you're doing that.

H.

At the end of the scene, **Liam** *races out through the barriers, barging past the* **Professional Man on Phone** *as he is pursued by the* **Uniformed Man**.

H.1

Group of Drunk Commuters (*cheer, laugh*)   Waaaaayyy!! / Go on my son! / It's Usain Bolt, look!

H.2

Commuter with Coffee (*knocked into by* **Liam**)   Oi, watch it fucking hell . . . –

Commuter's Pal   Christ, are you alright?

Commuter with Coffee   Wanker made me spill my coffee down my coat.

13.

Victoria Overground Station.

As **Liam** *is cornered and questioned by the* **Police**, *they are surrounded by a constant stream of people – commuters, theatre-goers, revellers, homeless, etc.*

Some of these people pass by individually, or in couples, or in small groups silently in varying paces.

But others are in dialogue/action as outlined below.

Throughout the scene, we hear noise from the traffic and general hubbub from the adjacent street, and the noise from inside the station – including the overhead tannoy.

Below are a selection of dialogues/actions which run simultaneously (though independently) from the main scene and each other.

Feel free to use all of them, none of them or some of them.

A.

A drunk **Commuter** *leans against a wall, eating a Burger King and fries from a brown paper bag.*

He occasionally checks his phone – tapping and scrolling.

Through the scene, the **Commuter** *manages to eat the entire burger and fries. Perhaps he's already halfway through at the top of the scene?*

When he has finished eating, he drops the brown paper bag (and its remaining contents) on the floor.

He remains where he is, checking his phone one last time before going inside the station, as a **Well-Dressed Woman** *enters and, passing by him, says . . .*

Well-Dressed Woman   Would you mind picking that up please?

Pause.

Well-Dressed Woman   I'm sorry, would you mind picking your litter up please?

Disgusting.

The **Well-Dressed Woman** *exits into the station.*

Pause.

The **Commuter** *finishes checking his phone, and exits into the station.*

B.

B.1

At the top of the scene, a **Friendly-Looking Couple**, *with bags, are talking to a* **Lady in Purple Uniform** *who is carrying a placard for 'London Bus Tours'.*

Lady in Purple Uniform   You need to go Piccadilly.

Friendly-Looking Man   Oh, really? Great great, we can do that.

Lady in Purple Uniform   Easiest way to get onto Regent Street's from Piccadilly Circus. Take the Victoria Line and change at Green Park.

Friendly-Looking Man   Victoria Line and change at Green Park.

Friendly-Looking Woman *elbows* **Friendly-Looking Man**.

Friendly-Looking Woman   I told you that didn't I?

Lady in Purple Uniform   It's the dark blue line. The pale blue's Victoria, you want the dark blue.

Friendly-Looking Man   Cool, great, we'll do that. What's your name again?

Friendly-Looking Woman *elbows* **Friendly-Looking Man**.

Friendly-Looking Woman   That's fine, thank you.

Lady in Purple Uniform   And just top up your Oyster card, it's cheaper that way.

The **Lady in Purple Uniform** *moves across the concourse, carrying the placard.*

B.2

She eventually makes it to the **Gent in Purple Uniform**, *who is sipping a coffee, watching the passers-by.*

On placing the placard down . . .

Lady in Purple Uniform   Thanks for your help, Alex.

Gent in Purple Uniform   Don't mention it.

Lady in Purple Uniform   How long have we got, half an hour?

Gent in Purple Uniform   I got you a coffee, here.

Gent in Purple Uniform *picks up a coffee he's left standing on the ground by his feet and passes it to the* **Lady in Purple Uniform**.

She takes it . . .

Lady in Purple Uniform   Any sugar in this?

Gent in Purple Uniform *gestures 'two'.*

Lady in Purple Uniform   Good for something then. What's going on there?

Gent in Purple Uniform *shrugs, and they drink their coffees in silence, watching passers-by.*

Long pause.

Gent in Purple Uniform   I'll go and see if Bob's back.

Lady in Purple Uniform   Okay.

The **Gent in Purple Uniform** *exits.*

The **Lady in Purple Uniform** *stays by the placard, sipping her drink.*

Long pause, until she is approached by **Two Older American Tourists** (*see below*).

B.3

Towards the end of the scene, **Two Older American Tourists** (*a couple*) *enter the concourse. They are dragging holdalls, one of them holds a map.*

One of them points to the **Lady in Purple Uniform** (*who is sipping her coffee*) *and they approach her.*

Tourist   Hi, sorry. The coach station?

Lady in Purple Uniform   Turn left there, Buckingham Palace Road. Follow it all the way down.

Tourist   Buckingham Palace Road?

Lady in Purple Uniform   Follow it all the way down to the traffic lights.

Tourist   Okay, great.

Tourist #2   Thank you very much.

The **Two Tourists** *exit, dragging their holdalls.*

B.4

Meanwhile, The **Friendly-Looking Couple**, *immediately following their enquiry with the Lady in Purple Uniform, hesitate briefly, then exit. The* **Friendly-Looking Woman** *leads the way, with the following dialogue as they go . . .*

Friendly-Looking Woman   I knew I shouldn't have listened to you. Why did I do that?

Friendly-Looking Man   Well, at least we know now. At least we're not in a specific rush . . . –

Friendly-Looking Woman   We should have asked as soon as we got out at St Pancras.

Friendly-Looking Man   It's fine, it's fine.

Friendly-Looking Man *kisses* **Friendly-Looking Woman** *on the head.*

Friendly-Looking Man   At least we definitely know now.

Friendly-Looking Woman   You can carry my bags when we get on the tube.

C.

C.1

There are three or four or more **Smokers** *standing on their own in isolated spots. They are smoking their first or second or more cigarettes before they exit into the station to get their trains.*

Some are young, some are old. Some are in suits, some aren't.

Some are looking at their phones, some are listening to music on their phones with headphones.

Maybe one of them is just watching the passers-by, deep in thought.

One *– maybe two? – of the* **Smokers** *stub out their cigarettes and exit to get their trains in the course of the scene.*

C.2

At the top of the scene, a terribly dishevelled **Homeless Man***, holding the butt of a roll-up in his clenched fist, wanders the area, sizing up the* **Smokers***.*

Long pause, as he does so.

Mid-way through the scene, the **Homeless Man** *approaches one of the* **Smokers***, who is texting on his/her phone.*

The **Homeless Man** *stands directly in front of the* **Smoker***.*

Homeless   Give me one smoke?

The **Homeless Man** *gestures with his clenched fist/roll-up.*

Pause.

Homeless   Cigarette, please.

Pause.

Homeless   Please.

The **Smoker** *turns his/her back on the* **Homeless Man***.*

The **Homeless Man** *follows him/her round and gestures.*

Homeless Please.

Smoker Sorry, nah, I can't help you.

Homeless One. One cigarette, please.

Smoker I can't help you, sorry.

The **Homeless Man** *hesitates, then walks off.*

Pause.

The **Homeless Man** *approaches a* **Second Smoker** *who is wearing headphones.*

The **Homeless Man** *gestures with his fist/roll-up.*

The **Second Smoker** *shakes his head.*

Homeless Please.

Pause.

Homeless Please . . . –

Second Smoker Last one, mate, last one.

The **Homeless Man** *retreats from the* **Second Smoker***.*

He wanders the space, sizing up the smokers, until he eventually exits.

D.

A **Drunk Woman** *in her work clothes, leaning against a wall.*

She is tap-tapping on her iPhone and smoking a cigarette.

A **Male Commuter** *stands close by, with a free newspaper under his arm, occasionally checking his watch.*

As the scene progresses, the **Male Commuter** *edges close to the* **Drunk Woman***.*

Long pause.

Male Commuter Nice.

Pause.

Male Commuter   Very nice.

Drunk Woman   Hm?

Male Commuter   What you're wearing, very nice.

Drunk Woman   Oh . . . –

Male Commuter   Sight for sore eyes.

Drunk Woman *nods, and returns to her iPhone.*

The **Male Commuter** *edges away, and checks his watch again.*

E.

Five young woman, dressed up for the night and drunk, enter, passing through the scene quickly.

Girl #1   . . . through the queue and straight to the front won't we?

Girl #2   Who do you know there again?

Girl #3   Kelly knows everyone there, she like must have been there nearly a hundred times or something.

Girl #1   'Shake it off, shake it off, oh oh.' – Jesus Christ, I am . . . –

Girl #5   Steaming, yeah, these shoes.

Girl #1/Girl #4   'Shake it off, shake it off, oh oh.'

Girl #5   Breaking my ankles, fuck. Fuck, hold on a minute!

They exit.

F.

At some point in the scene, three **Blokes** *in their late twenties, dressed up for a night out, pass through the concourse. They are also a bit drunk, a bit loud.*

Bloke #1   . . . says she wants a handbag, I'm like 'alright, yeah'. Turns out it's six hundred fucking pound or more, I'm like 'what?' Six hundred for a bag, mate, yeah, like when the fuck did that happen?

Bloke #3   Ludicrous.

Bloke #2   Should take her up the Shard or something.

Bloke #1   'Course you've got to do it haven't you? Gotta fucking spend it or I'll never hear the end, I'm like 'alright, love, alright, whatever you want . . .'

At which point, they've gone.

G.

Mid-way through the scene, another **Tourist** *enters the concourse, dragging a holdall.*

He/she stops, and sits on top of the holdall. He/she takes a packet of wet-wipes from his/her pocket.

She/he wipes her hands and face vigorously.

She/he puts the wet-wipes away.

She/he stands and takes the holdall.

She/he exits.

H.

At some point in the scene, two female **Shoppers**, *carrying shopping bags, enter and make their way into the station, with the following dialogue.*

Shopper #1   – . . . that's nice, yeah. Really lovely that, Tam, yeah.

Shopper #2   I thought she could wear it this weekend or something.

Shopper #1   The sparkles and everything, they're nice.

Shopper #2   Yeah, and with her pink skirt? You know the pink skirt with the stripes down the side?

Shopper #1   That's good quality that is. Top Shop is it?

Shopper #2   H & M. I mean, she's grown so much I could probably squeeze into it myself. Interesting.

Shopper #1   Could be interesting, yeah. Just make sure you leave the tags on, you know what they're like.

I.

At some point in the scene, a **Grandmother** *with her* **Daughter in her thirties** *and her* **Teenage Daughter** *(who are holding hands) cross the concourse. The* **Grandmother** *is smoking. The* **Teenage Daughter** *wears a 'Billy Elliot' t-shirt under her sparkly cardigan. They are dressed up to go to the theatre.*

Daughter in her thirties   This way, it's across the road over there. You see the sign?

Grandmother   Quite like a piss before we go in if that's alright.

Daughter in her thirties   Well, we've got a good five minutes before it starts. – Cheer up, it's *Billy Elliot*, look. Thought you were looking forward to it.

Teenage Daughter   Yeah, mega.

Grandmother   What's wrong with her now?

. . . and they are gone.

J.

Station-Commuter-On-Phone #1   – . . . You're funny, yeah, in a nice way. . . . You've a nice way about you . . . – No, well, I don't know, you'll have to find out. – . . . Come and find out for yourself, I'll show you around.

. . . Yeah . . . What, sorry, tours? . . . Tours, no, that's a euphemism. Do you know what a euphemism is? . . . –

There's keys . . . – Set of keys that get passed around, we have this . . . –

Agreement really, it's an unspoken agreement really. . . . No, during recess . . . Recess, yeah . . . – Well they call it recess, but it's a nightmare until after conference . . . Yeah, I know, thank god . . .

Thank god that's over with. – No, that's fine . . . It's fine, yeah, everything still stands. Who have you got for me? Anyone new?

. . . Okay. . . . Okay, yeah, sounds tasty . . . Sounds right up my street, Michael, yeah . . . Well, you know me . . . – Long days, long nights, not too much energy . . . Someone who'll do the grafting, right . . . – You know me, yeah. Pay the bills, keep the kids in school . . . – Kids, mortgage, constituents. Well, there's that at least . . . – Sarcasm . . . – Well, course you're not surprised, why the fuck would you be? . . . You know I missed my train already. . . . Twenty minutes . . . Twenty minutes, straight to bed, be a good boy . . . – So, make the call then . . . Make the call, Michael, you know I like a new face . . . – Surprise me then.

15.

Oxford Street, Sports Direct store.

As **Liam** *enters and has his encounter with the Sports Direct* **Security Guard**, *there are, simultaneously, a number of dialogues and actions stationed-in, or travelling through, the scene.*

Feel free to use all, or none, or some of the scenes/moments.

A.

Another Homeless Person *is asleep on the pavement, covered almost entirely by a sleeping bag.*

Sometime during the scene, a **Smart Passer-By** *enters, headphones in ears.*

The **Smart Passer-By** *exits.*

Pause.

The **Smart Passer-By** *re-enters, the way he came.*

He stops by **Another Homeless Person**.

He throws the packet of cigarettes onto him/her.

The **Smart Passer-By** *turns and exits.*

Another Homeless Person *sleeps.*

B.

A distance away from the central scene, a middle-aged black man – **Preacher** *– is standing on the corner of the street, holding a microphone attached to a portable speaker that is slung over his shoulder.*

He holds Jehovah's Witness leaflets in one hand.

Stacked against the shop-front, next to him, are leaflets and books.

Preacher   – . . . and in the television, online, work – in all these things, they don't let god into your heart. Because one day you are going to wake up. One day you will wake up and stand before the judgemancy of god, when you are about your ashes, when you are dead. –

As the **Preacher** *continues, a* **Drunk Young Man** *enters, puffing on a Vapouriser.*

He stops close to the **Preacher**, *leaning on a rail or a wall, and scrutinises him.*

Preacher   – And as you hear the goodness, as you hear the gospel in your heart, you will say that I am sorry. And God, the grace of God, the new God, he sees that it is not your fault, because what you are doing you don't know that it is wrong. And the Bible say whatever you sow, you sow into life, and into that body. But if you destroy that body, when you want to use that body then that body has gone for you.

Do as our forefathers used to believe when they taught their children to fear God, for the fear of God is our joy, and we are only here for a moment.

The **Drunk Young Man** *moves closer and swipes a leaflet from the* **Preacher**, *then exits, passing along the street, as the* **Preacher** *continues . . .*

Preacher Yes, my friend, we are passing through. You can be here today, tomorrow, no more. And then it will be too late to find God, it will be too late. And that's why you have to make a decision of your life. Because there's no repentance in the grave. When you die, that's no repentance again. So you need to make a decision of your life, before it's too late. Jesus is not coming back again to go to the cross, you have to make a decision. Of heaven or hell, life or death, death or life, it's over to you. You have in this life, the decision . . . –

C.

Sometime during the scene, a middle-aged **Hen Party** *of four, and one camp* **Male Companion**, *pass across the space. Three of the* **Hen Party** *and the* **Male Companion** *are singing Adele's 'Someone Like You' drunkenly to the* **Hen Bride**.

Hen Bride (*as the others sing*) You're mental, all of you . . . / Mental, give over now.

/ Oh god, I knew this was a bad idea. / Stop it, it's embarrassing. / Can't we go home now?

D.

Sometime during the scene, two **Smartly Dressed Brothers** *pass through the space, talking.*

Brother #1 – . . . essentially he's a horror director. *Funny Games*, *The White Ribbon*, even something like *Amour* follows the traditional slasher narrative.

Brother #2 *Funny Games* being the most explicit.

Brother #1   It's basically *Halloween* for the art-house crowd.

Brother #2   *Hidden*.

Brother #1   *Hidden*, yeah, I love that film. Daniel Auteuil.

Brother #2   Daniel Auteuil, brilliant.

Brother #1   You know I took Mum to the Curzon Soho to see that?

Brother #2   She jumped out her seat.

Brother #1   She literally jumped out her seat, you remember?

Brother #2   No, I don't know where I was, probably working, you told me later I think.

That bit.

Brother #1   That bit, yeah. Have you watched the *Nymphomaniac* blu-ray yet?

Brother #2   It's on Netflix, no I haven't.

And they've gone . . . –

E.

Sometime during the scene, four adolescents – two girls and two boys – on a double date, pass through the scene.

They are dressed appropriately for dating.

The **First Couple***, who are getting on quite well, arms over each other, lead the way.*

The **Second Couple***, who aren't getting on so well, lag behind.*

E.1

The **First Couple** *. . .*

Girl #1   Nah, I never said that, just . . .

Boy #2   What, not even a little bit?

Girl #1 You think I'm weird.

Boy #2 Weird? Nah, piss off I don't.

Girl #1 I like get myself all obsessed with it.

Boy #2 Reckon you're going to love it down Opium. Brilliant.

E.2

The **Second Couple**.

Pause.

Boy #1 Chewing gum?

Girl #2 Nah, you're alright.

Pause.

Boy #1 Cold sort of.

Girl #2 Yeah, I suppose. Suppose it's quite cold. You alright?

Boy #1 Yeah, fine.

F.

A worn-out **Refuse Collector** *pushes his large wheelie bin-cart to one of the street bins.*

He pulls the green bin-liner out of the street bin and empties it into his wheelie bin.

A **Passer-By** *drops a half-full can of Coke into the wheelie bin as he/she passes.*

The **Refuse Collector** *continues emptying the street bin.*

G.

At the top of the scene, a **Middle Eastern-Looking Man** *stands by a shop-front.*

He has his mobile phone at his ear, waiting for an answer.

Pause.

He puts the phone down.

Long pause.

He dials the phone number and waits for an answer.

Pause, then . . .

Middle Eastern-Looking Man (*on phone*)   . . . There you are, I was stressing out man . . . Where? . . . – Yeah, well I'm in the same spot . . . – I said I'm in the same spot . . . – You've got what, pizza slices? . . . Nah, pizza's good . . . – Grab some Ben & Jerry's . . . – Ben & Jerry's, anything . . . – Alright, see you in a minute then, I'll be here . . . I'll be here, yeah.

H.

At some point during the scene, three **Suited & Booted Blokes** *run past, out of breath, in a hurry. Two of them are in better health than the other.*

Suited & Booted Bloke #1 (*as they run*)   Come on, there's still time for one more if we're quick! / Yeah, we will, think positive!

Suited & Booted Bloke #2 (*as they run*)   / We're never going to make it, what you on?!

Suited & Booted Bloke #3 (*slowing down, pulling his phone out of his pocket*)   Give me a minute, yeah?! I'll catch you up, my phone!

I.

At some point in the scene, four or five **Fashionable-Looking Students** *walk past. They are laughing, giggling at* **Student #1***'s rant. They have cans of lager, and some are smoking.*

Student #1 (*as they pass, laughing*)   . . . probably getting a nosh off another pig isn't he? Cameron one end, Osborne ejaculating all over the other while Boris wanks himself stupid in the corner. Coked-up, flicking each other's bell-ends to see who's got the shiniest jap.

CPSIA information can be obtained
at www.ICGtesting.com
Printed in the USA
FFOW04n1754290616
25499FF